Inspirational Writing
for Academic Publication

Gillie Bolton with Stephen Rowland

Los Angeles | London | New Delhi
Singapore | Washington DC

Los Angeles | London | New Delhi
Singapore | Washington DC

SAGE Publications Ltd
1 Oliver's Yard
55 City Road
London EC1Y 1SP

SAGE Publications Inc.
2455 Teller Road
Thousand Oaks, California 91320

SAGE Publications India Pvt Ltd
B 1/I 1 Mohan Cooperative Industrial Area
Mathura Road
New Delhi 110 044

SAGE Publications Asia-Pacific Pte Ltd
3 Church Street
#10-04 Samsung Hub
Singapore 049483

Editor: Marianne Lagrange
Editorial assistant: Rachael Plant
Production editor: Thea Watson
Copyeditor: Jane Robson
Proofreader: Jill Birch
Marketing manager: Catherine Slinn
Cover design: Naomi Robinson
Typeset by: C&M Digitals (P) Ltd, Chennai, India
Printed in India by Replika Press Pvt Ltd

Library of Congress Control Number: 2013950808

British Library Cataloguing in Publication data

A catalogue record for this book is available from
the British Library

ISBN 978-1-4462-8236-6
ISBN 978-1-4462-8237-3 (pbk)

Contents

About the Authors

Dr Gillie Bolton is an international authority on writing and author of a long publication list including nine books (one in 4th edition), academic papers (many in top-ranking journals), as well as professional articles, poetry, and for a lay readership. She has peer-reviewed for many journals and has been a long-serving editor of an academic and two professional journals.

Stephen Rowland, Emeritus Professor of University College London, is author of four books on the nature of research and learning in a range of contexts, and has particularly enjoyed supervising and examining doctoral students. He has been a founding and long-term editor of a leading international journal and has a wide experience of research across disciplinary boundaries.

Acknowledgements

Gillie and Stephen are grateful to colleagues, course members, students, friends and family who have helped us share the gift of how to write well through this publication. These include Tony Harland, Otago University, Amanda Gilbert, Victoria University, Barbara Grant, Auckland University (all New Zealand); David McCormack, Orla Hanratty and other valued colleagues at National University of Ireland Maynooth; Jane Wilde, Lesley Boydell and the rest of the wonderful Institute for Public Health, Ireland team; Claire Collins, Lynley Deaker, Megan Fidler, Ronan Foley, Robert Hamberger, Paula Hayden, Bernadette Knewstubb, Erika Löfström, Arlene McDowell, Erika Mansnerus, Margaret Meyer, Richard Roche, Tracy Rohan, Clare Shephard, Kerry Shephard, Rob Wass, Joan Williams; all those who generously sent us their writing to quote, but did not want their full names included; and many health and medical academics and professionals in Sheffield, Nottingham and London. And we gratefully acknowledge the help of Sue Clegg, Barbara Grant, Alison Farrell and Claire Aichison. Our grateful thanks go to Marianne Lagrange, as always a wonderful editor to work with, and Rachael Plant, Thea Watson and Kathryn Bromwich for all their helpful support at Sage. We also thank Dan Rowland for essential computer advice and Alice Watson for redrawing Stephen's diagram so beautifully (see next page), Flynn Rowland, Amber, and Ivy Watson for their understanding when Grannie and Grandpa were sitting boringly at the computer and not playing.

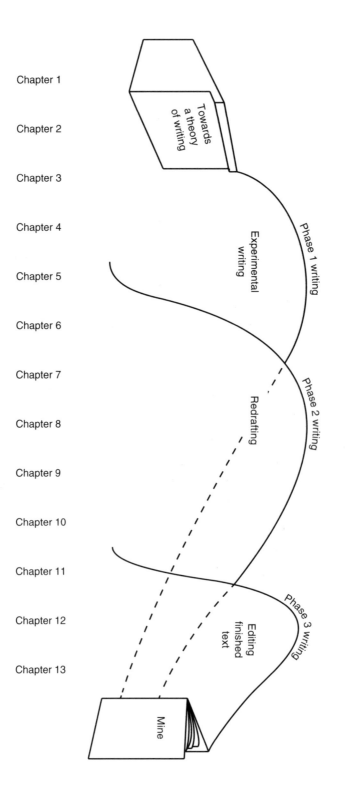

The journey from research to publication

Chapter 1

Chapter 2

Chapter 3

Chapter 4

Chapter 5

Chapter 6

Chapter 7

Chapter 8

Chapter 9

Chapter 10

Chapter 11

Chapter 12

Chapter 13

Towards a theory of writing

Experimental writing

Phase 1 writing

Phase 2 writing

Redrafting

Phase 3 writing

Editing finished text

Mine

Starting Out

1

How to Read this Book

Inspirational Writing shows how writing research publications can, at its best, be itself a critical process of reflection and re-evaluation. Writing can enable us to enquire into research processes, and clearly articulate arguments and theories. Through writing we form our scholarly identity and intellectual selves, developing what we know, understand, think and feel. *Inspirational Writing* gives a lucid route through the processes of writing for academic publication.

Writing can become exhilarating as we find eloquent expression for what we want and need to say concisely and with precision. And then we can communicate it confidently to those who will understand and appreciate it. If it's inspirational to write, it will be inspirational to read; if a boring slog to write, it will be a boring slog to read. If musicians play, why can't we writers?

All the information and advice in *Inspirational Writing* is from the experience of Gillie and Stephen's long careers of academic writing, editing, reviewing, PhD supervision and examining, and latterly, teaching 'academic writing for publication' courses/retreats. Here are some responses from participants on those courses:

> My preconceptions were really challenged.
>
> It was an introduction to a completely different approach to writing which solved my main writing difficulties.
>
> I gave myself affirmation that I can find a style of my own and that is a key to being a good writer.
>
> I have been given lots of mechanisms to loosen up my approach, and LOTS of tips about making the process more manageable.
>
> (Academic writing course members)

Stephen

As a journal editor I have often wished for a book to inspire academics to become writers who take pleasure in the creation of the stories of their research. Written with such experienced and new academics in mind – as well as PhD students whom we see as a budding academics – *Inspirational Writing* aims to meet that need.

We have not attempted to meet the needs of PhD students for help specifically related to thesis writing: that is readily available from libraries, the internet and many books covering such issues as plagiarism, referencing methods, basic grammar or the simple questions of structure that relate to essay writing or other tasks set by tutors.

We assume that the reader of this book is already a competent researcher. Writing is itself a process of discovery and so cannot be completely divorced from issues of research methodology. We have tried, however, to take a wide approach and not to tread upon the toes of those in the disciplines caught up in important methodological debate. The book 'wears its theory lightly' as one helpful reviewer put it.

We wished to give our attention to academic writing because we realised so much bad writing is caused by fear and lack of understanding of its processes, a finding echoed by Stephen King about fiction (2000: 127). This fear leads some academics to write with a conspicuous lack of authority, and as a consequence their texts tend to appear pompous and inscrutable.

> All hide behind the idea that unintelligible prose indicates a sophisticated mind ... [Yet] awful indecipherable [academic] prose is its own form of armour, protecting the fragile, sensitive thoughts of timid souls. (Limerick, 1993: 24)

A useful approach to this problem is to reflect:

> Who is in charge? Am I in charge of my own writing? Or is my writing in charge of me, or perhaps some imaginary judge from my past is in control, and I am merely a passenger? If I am not in the driving seat, why aren't I?

My study of good and bad writing started with George Orwell's *Why I Write* ([1946] 1984), which he managed to make engaging, funny and eminently readable.

Authors and readers have begun publicly to vent frustration that critical writing uses unreadable, 'strangulated and pretentious' language (Grey and Sinclair, 2006: 445), severely restricting readership to an exclusive few. And there is a wider public concern that academics should communicate their research more effectively across disciplinary and social boundaries (Rowland, 2006). Organisations such as the international Wellcome Trust promotes health research and public engagement with that research. We even have a rising class of 'celebrity academics' who regularly appear on television and other public media in an attempt to address this need. While we do not expect our readers to aspire to celebrity status, and there is much that is problematic about such a notion, we do agree that academic writing should develop ways of more widely communicating its research.

There are approaches to writing that can achieve this:

> The writing we like doesn't just tell people things in a didactic way, it opens a door for an experience to be had by the reader. Good writing is suggestive and pungent, it evokes feelings – relief, recognition, drama, disdain, horror – and bodily responses – the flush of recognition and the sharp intake of breath, the tingle as we feel that this might be showing us something we hadn't thought or experienced before. Good writing is often unpredictable – shocking in its terseness or economy, audacious in its sudden sweep or the intimacy of a confidence. Our concern is that very little writing in our field has these qualities. … We want writing to be taken seriously, as powerful and evocative performance, able to change peoples' experiences of the world, rather than as a shriven, cowed and cowering path towards routinised, professionalised 'publication'. We wonder if it is possible to write differently. (Grey and Sinclair, 2006: 452)

It is not only possible, but imperative to write differently. It is exhilarating when we've managed to say what we mean, and mean what we say: clearly, succinctly and inspirationally. At other times it's tougher, but then intellectual endeavour and enquiry is hard work. Hopefully, having worked through this, no writer will feel that 'Writing a book is a horrible, exhausting struggle, like a long bout of some painful illness' (Orwell, 1984: 10).

Inspirational Writing gives clear developmental phases which can be followed in order, or used in ways appropriate to each writer. The chapters are set out according to these three phases; they make perfect sense read in any order, however, according to the preference of individual readers. Reading the first three chapters first would however be most supportive.

We only learn how to write by writing. Stephen and I recommend doing the exercises included both within the text, and at chapter ends. If you only have time for a few, please try the ones all our academic writing course members found most powerful:

- Expressing the essence of the work in one sentence (pp. 110–11, 113)
- Writing letters to and from
  - readers (pp. 61–2)
  - internal mentor (pp. 50, 58, 82–3, 91)
  - internal terrorist (pp. 83, 91)
- Reordering sentences and paragraphs and sections (particularly paragraphs) (Chapter 11)

The further readings at the end of each chapter include some texts giving straightforward practical advice, and some exploring much more theoretical aspects: all drawn from a wide range of disciplines. We suggest reading whatever seems interesting and useful: this book does not assume readers read the lot.

When we come across academic writing in the future (we're both retired), we hope to hear how writers really enjoy the processes of writing and perceive the actual writing as research in itself. There will be no further need for such as the *Journal of Philosophy and Literature*'s Bad Writing contest: nominations for the competition were solicited on the internet, and the final tally broadcast. The public caught the joke about academic writing being helpfully exposed. The fourth annual winning sentence was:

> The move from a structuralist account in which capital is understood to structure social relations in relatively homologous ways to a view of hegemony in which power relations are subject to repetition, convergence, and rearticulation brought the question of temporality into the thinking of structure, and marked a shift from a form of Althusserian theory that takes structural totalities as theoretical objects to one in which the insights into the contingent possibility of structure inaugurate a renewed conception of hegemony as bound up with the contingent sites and strategies of the rearticulation of power.
>
> (Judith Butler, quoted Bauerlein, 2004: 191)

Eubanks and Schaeffer (2008) on the other hand make something of a defence of academic writing, based on the writing of the American philosopher Harry Frankfurt.

Inspirational Writing is written as a dialogue with different voices offering a range of perspectives and strategies. I, Gillie Bolton, take you my reader, through all the stages and phases, giving explanations, examples and exercises. Stephen Rowland consistently chips in with advice from his own wide and lengthy experience as author of several books and many papers, journal editor, PhD supervisor and examiner. The voices of other authorities in the field and our own academic writing course members, add richness where appropriate.

There are also four fictional academics, whom we created to contribute sections of their reflective research journals. They tussle with the writing problems presented in each chapter. These two women and two men, at different stages in their careers, are based on the many academic colleagues and students we have worked with over our long careers. We imagined them reading the draft of *Inspirational Writing*, undertaking the writing exercises, and reflecting on their ongoing problems in their research journals. Their journal extracts raise issues and problems at the start of each chapter, and are responded to and dealt with practically and critically in that chapter. So these monologues reliably inform you, our readers, what is in each chapter in a fuller way than any bullet list could. They also reinforce the learning from previous chapters.

We found Seamus, Helena, Lee, and Joseph's responses to our text really dynamic. It often felt as if they were nudging us to include significant elements which we'd missed. Or that their very human dilemmas and problems helped keep us on track. In an interesting way, they helped us do what we are recommending to you, our readers, as we went along. Here the characters introduce themselves with part of their responses to my first exercise, which follows their short pieces.

Seamus: Well that's it! I've just got to get my ideas together if ever I'm to make a mark in the kind of journal that will lead to my getting a chair before I'm 60. Pity I can't just do it by teaching, I so love talking to my third years and post grads about my thoughts on number theory. Why does research always have to be more important than teaching? Socrates didn't write! I think there's a lot of intellectual snobbery about research publications. I want to publish, but am not prepared to lose my values as a teacher.

Helena: Who am I, and where and how and why am I just now? Well I think I'm probably having a mid-life crisis (I'm 42). Am I right to want to change things now? I could stay in my job at the college, which is a good one, or I could really put my heart and soul into all the ideas which are winging around in my mind for this PhD about the role of humour in teaching painting, and then – dare I hope – become a lecturer at a really progressive thinking university, with a publication list. But as a painter, I'm a real beginner in writing, especially the academic sort, and need a lot of help.

Lee: OK. Me? I am here in Cambridge, actually a lecturer, but not with tenure. I want to make the best of the opportunity. Everything is so different from home here. My research? Genetics. It's all clear to me, but they say my written English is not always clear. Because I need to write up my research, that is what I need to work on. I've been invited to submit a paper. It is to a prestigious journal special issue. This is exciting, but I know I'm not ready.

Joseph: I'm very excited about my new postgrad contract. It really gives me the chance to extend the debates on 'after postmodernism' in the social sciences and make my mark. Not sure how this book will help, but it can't do any harm even if it is for people who lack my confidence in written argument and theory. I've not had much luck in publishing since my PhD, but I guess it's just a matter of time. I think my grasp of written English is pretty good even if it isn't my first language, but there does seem to be something rather stuffy about the way English academics write, which gets in the way of my flow of ideas, particularly when we're dealing with complex sociological conceptualizations, which can't just be summed up in short sentences and everyday words. Perhaps this book will help me solve this paradox.

Don't just read, WRITE!

Give yourself about ten minutes to write, set an alarm if that would help you to start straight away.

Answer these questions, quickly because you have little time:

- Who am I?
- What am I?
- How is my research and writing developing?
- Where am I working and writing?
- Why is my research important to me?
- When can I write, and when do I need to publish?

Reread it; note if there:

- is anything surprising in your responses;
- are any questions, if so answer them;
- is anything you are dissatisfied about; if so, write some more to develop your thinking;
- is anything practical your responses suggest you should do; if so do it.

And READ some more:

Eubanks, P. and Schaeffer, J.D. (2008) 'A kind word for bullshit: The problem of academic writing', *College Composition and Communication*, 59 (3): 372–88.

The language of academic publications has often been chided for being a kind of 'bullshit'. Here is a provocative discussion of the significance of 'bullshit' in academic writing, drawing upon the work of the American philosopher Harry Frankfurt. Eubank and Schaeffer make something of a defence of academic language.

King, S. (2000) *On Writing: A Memoir of the Craft.* New York: Simon & Schuster.
Stephen King writes engagingly, reflectively and valuably about the craft of writing: this is a book for all writers, not just fiction writers. And you do not have to be an admirer or even a reader of his fiction to gain much benefit from what King has to say.

Porter, S. (2010) *Inking the Deal: A Guide for Successful Academic Publication.* Waco, TX: Baylor University Press.
Porter presents insights and practical suggestions for both seasoned scholars and newly minted PhDs who have yet to develop an academic publishing profile. Written primarily for scholars in the arts and humanities, Porter's advice will help readers gain a valuable understanding of the publishing process and a new confidence with which to pursue academic success.

2

Towards a Theory of Writing

Writing for academic publication, like all writing, needs to inform clearly and straightforwardly, communicate effectively with its intended audience and have a form which encourages readers to continue right through to the end. This chapter gives some orientation to writing, and explains the three essential *Phases of Writing*, how they work together and how to work with them.

Seamus: I have no trouble talking to students about difficult ideas. But somehow writing it all out just feels sterile. There's no one there to listen and whenever I try to write my thoughts get all constipated. Where do I start? I like the idea of writing as a journey. The dotted lines on the map (p. viii) suggest that Phase 1 writing can continue at the same time as Phase 2, and then both of these parallel to Phase 3. That looks helpful, but what exactly is the difference between these kinds of writing?

Helena: I sit down to write and nothing comes; I just stare at a blank screen. Or else I start, and write complete rubbish, and delete it all. Or else I plan a writing day and end up answering all my emails until there is no time left for me to start. And everything I read is in such clever difficult language, I don't think I can ever write like that (do I really want to?). Unless I can be given a clear thorough enjoyable route through to writing, I can't do this PhD. This picture on p. viii looks as though I'm going to get that. But how can writing have a 'theory'? I know about theory in art; can it be at all similar? I'm scared. What can I do with such strong emotions in a dry place like a university?

Lee: I need to get a single author publication. I've always collaborated before. I tried to do exactly what the editors of the special issue of a prestigious journal asked (the list of instructions was very long). But they returned my draft covered in red. They said my research looks very exciting, but my 'discussion' section does not give any more than the 'findings' section'. What does that mean? I tried really hard to do what they said they wanted. Can learning about a 'theory of writing' and going through all the lengthy stages shown on the graph (p. viii) really help me?

Joseph: I'm looking forward to getting an idea of what this 'theory' of writing is. The diagram suggests it's a kind of process theory. But the overlapping hills suggest it's not exactly a 'one step at a time' kind of thing.

Writing doesn't need to be done in a specific 'academic' way to be acceptable and successful. It doesn't need the teeth to be gritted, the shoulders hunched and the forehead furrowed. A degree of failure is not inevitable before most writers have even started: good academic writers are made and not born (most of them). And the aim of this book is to make good academic writers.

Orientation

Many of us have such a pile of fears and memories from school teachers, supervisors, tutors and imaginary instructors who niggle away in our brains saying there is a proper way to write and structure a piece of academic writing, and it's nothing like what I am putting down on the page now. Yet there is an assumption that all academics know how to write, and are expected just to get on with creating wonderful papers. We can probably all echo John Henry Newman's experience that, when he started writing, his idea 'plunged into a thicket, curled itself up like a hedgehog, or changed colours like a chameleon' (Hurley, 2013: 31).

We set out on writing like a traveller with so much baggage – we are unable to enjoy the journey itself because we are longing to arrive and put the suitcases, bags and rucksacks down. And we are unable to look around and gain benefit from the places we pass through and people we meet. Writing needn't be like that. *Inspirational Writing* helps reduce our luggage to the essential only. The journey can be divided into sections; only the stuff essential for the current leg of the journey need be carried at any one time. This really is light enjoyable travelling.

Written texts help to influence and structure the world, so at the same time, we are right to take the job really seriously and get anxious about it. And it is appropriate we wish to take time to understand the process to get it as right as possible, by reading books like this perhaps.

> Previously I have held back from writing, feeling I could keep it all in my head, come up with the answer and then write out my thoughts 'perfectly'. What proved immensely helpful from our meeting was to turn this on its head and *just write!* By returning to my scribbly mess at a later stage, I have managed to unravel some valid and useful points.
>
> (Claire Collins)

The very process of writing helps to produce creative ideas and insight, as Claire found. Struggling to write about something, whether a weighty theory, a puzzling event, or to communicate a feeling in a personal letter, is one of the best pathways to beginning to make sense of it.

Most authors are, I think, like Claire and me in needing to write a 'scribbly mess', which we can work on to create the finished piece. This process of working, from scribbles to polished manuscript, is much less easy to observe than the working of a painter from sketchbook experiments to canvas. Although I am no painter, when I go to an exhibition showing painters' sketchbooks, I can relate to their process because I can see it. We don't generally see writers' processes.

We can be forgiven therefore for finding learning to write difficult. All these complex processes are undertaken in private, in camera even. I could learn from watching a joiner make a cupboard, a dry-stone-waller carefully select a rock and gently work it into place, or a surgeon excise a tumour, but I can't instructively watch someone write. And the nature of the finished product generally gives no indication of the struggles and deletions of its drafts. In fact it is a common misconception that a well set out, helpfully illustrated clear argument flowed from its writer's pen in that way from the start. There might be gifted authors who can do that; most are probably more like Dickens, whose manuscripts show deletions, insertions and rewriting (sadly the magazine episode nature of their publication meant he never reshaped his novels structurally, which would have made them even stronger).

Stephen

When I started out as a researcher it never occurred to me that I could write differently. I considered that I wrote with accuracy and precision in a logical and clear manner. I later realised that this writing was shaped not only by my school experience as a student of sciences, but by my training to be an army officer. The latter was even more formal in its approach than the former. For example, I was taught that the instructions an officer gives to his men prior to battle (an 'orders group') are written under the headings: Situation, Mission, Execution, Logistics, Command and Signals, Any questions. When I later trained as a school teacher, the degree of formality of lesson plans was rather similar.

I wrote in a similarly clear and ordered fashion as I set out on my research, which involved close observations of children in a primary classroom. I was fortunate that Michael, my more experienced co-researcher, came from an arts and humanities background. He pointed out (and I could readily see this) that, although my accounts of the children were very clear and ordered, his were much more open and speculative, raising questions, allowing interesting digressions and, as a consequence, providing a much richer account of the situations which we had both observed. While such writing would have been useless for issuing orders to soldiers before battle (where command and control is what matters), it seemed much more appropriate for ethnographic field-notes aimed to stimulate our further discussion.

I soon found that writing in this more open way was much more enjoyable. It enabled me to recall things I had observed but forgotten about, stimulated me to construct all sorts of hypotheses about the way the children I was observing were thinking, and appeared to be much more engaging for my co-researcher.

A couple of years later, when my co-researcher published a book of our research (Armstrong, 1980) I was happy to find my field-notes, with little or no further editing, provided the account and discussion of many of our observations.

Inspiration

This book gives the what, how, for whom, where, when, and of course the why, of the whole process of academic writing. It explains how to dive into writing (Claire's *'just write!'*), unhampered by fears of that judge's red pen. It suggests how writing can enable us to re-experience the excitement of what we feel, think, know, believe. And to be able to communicate inspirational material, ideas, theories to readers. Listen to how others responded to those activities:

> I unexpectedly got to the core of some deep held beliefs.
>
> I found the exercises engaged me in a process of thinking much more deeply.
>
> (Academic writing course members)

Inspirational Writing shows that a myriad of forms are not only acceptable to editors and readers, but welcomed: they do not want to be bored. Many routes and strategies make the process enjoyable (yes, you heard right: enjoy-able), stimulating and inspirational to both writer and reader. The myth of academic writing being mysterious and needing a wizard's arts, is exploded. All the phases and stages are explained in an upbeat way, and suggestions are made for exercises which seem more like games: playshops rather than workshops.

There is no one way to write academically. People are very different, so we are all different writers. Our ways of working and being with our writing, data and theories are different. There is one imperative, however. To return to the metaphor above: there is one essential piece of luggage needed on all writing journeys. This is a positive attitude to writing. Whatever the discipline, our readers want to be drawn into the argument, theory and data. If our research and writing fires us, it will inspire our readers. If I respect myself as a writer, then my readers will respect my writing. If I can trust the writing process as outlined in this book, then I will create trustworthy writing. Good writing results from each of us being able to:

- respect ourselves as writers and researchers;
- trust the process of writing to enable us to find what we need to say, and express it fully, clearly and succinctly;
- be generous enough to give ourselves the gift of quality focused time to do it in.

This attitude enables each writer to listen to the authority of their own knowledge, experience, and wisdom, rather than trying to write for an examiner or teacher who knows better. In taking on this self-respectful, trusting, generous attitude we pay respect to the type of writers we are, rather than trying to force ourselves into perceived moulds. Everything else hangs on this. Once I am in this attitude, I am listening to the authority of my own knowledge, experience and wisdom. So I am keen to get the ramifications of what I have to say down in a form which communicates clearly and expressively to my reader. In so doing, I also pay respect to my reader, trusting them to do their part in meeting me in my writing, because they perceive me to be communicating with them appropriately. A positive attitude leads writers to bring:

- enthusiasm, creativity and heartfelt feelings;
- willingness to communicate properly with readers;
- care with editing.

In this, academic writing is no different from any other writing genre. We will write well if we write with commitment, and as interestingly as we think, and also as interested in our readers as we are in those with whom we converse orally. We allow ourselves to do this by developing our own individual voices with their own communicating power. Each writer finding their voice, and learning how to use it with confidence, is significant in the struggle to write well: this is what enables them to say what they mean comprehensibly and clearly, and to mean what they say. 'Writing is drawing the essence of what we know out of the shadows' (Knausgaard, quoted in Cusk, 2013: 2). As academic researchers we are inspired by a passion for our ideas and findings and a desire to share them; if not we would seek other work. Perceiving 'writing up' this research as drudgery will necessarily result in boring publications, almost as painful to read as they were to write.

> I was pleased to have the stigma of academic writing challenged by encouraging individual expression (as it should be, rather than format-conforming prose). It challenges the fog-factor academic writing that is seen as natural.
>
> (Academic writing course member)

When I was a student my supervisor set essay titles: questions to which I had to write the answer. This was not a genuine dialogue however, as my lecturers knew the answers they wanted from me, and I had no power or authority in the way I wrote. Now it's different: I want to say something important and original and in my own way, with my own authority. I am in a position of power as an academic writer. Remembering this all the way through the writing process enhances it greatly. The function of editors and peer reviewers (and doctoral supervisors and examiners) is to assist me to write as well and interestingly as I can, including as much original data and material as possible.

Three Phases of Writing for Publication

Academic writing can helpfully be thought of as involving three different approaches or phases. A key to successful and positive writing is undertaking them all. The role of each phase is clear, simple and straightforward to grasp and practise.

1 Write for yourself to find out what you know, think, feel and want to say.
2 Redraft to communicate with your reader.
3 Edit for posterity to offer clarity, clear language, structure, grammar, correct references ...

Each of these phases involves the writer in critical thinking and research (albeit different kinds of research). Each phase and stage develops the argument, the theory, as well as the exposition of the facts; none of the phases merely reports.

I give these phases in order 1–3: working through them in this order is valuable. Writers, however, move through these phases in very different ways. Some work straight through and complete, as if the phases were steps.

Most revisit earlier phases to revitalise their writing as they go through: it is often a dynamically reiterative process. Many writers return to Phase 1 again with new material to insert into the text; they then work on this new writing through Phases 2 and 3. Some, moreover, do some of the initial phase in their heads, only writing when they are fairly clear what they want to say. Leaving out a phase, though, can make a publication dull, muddled, incomplete and prevent it speaking to the appropriate audience.

Phase 1: Write for myself to find out what I know, think, feel, and want to say

Phase 1 is explorative, tentative and uncertain: Claire's 'scribbled mess'. The only thing that matters now is the content of what we jam down on the page: grammar, proper construction, intellectual ways of expressing stuff 'properly' are dealt with in Phases 2 and 3. What matters is that we now capture valuable content. We search for our theory by reflecting freely, as well as reflecting upon the data, and by sifting in an unfocused way through the literature (journal papers, books, internet sites, etc.) for material which informs the development of ideas and offers examples. This experimental and explorative stage enables me to grasp what I think, and what my data and research are telling me; it enables me to draw upon the wealth of my experience with a width and depth no other process can offer.

This phase is essentially relatively unfocused; a vital attitude enabling the capturing of insight, as well as marshalling thoughts and theories. One of the reasons academic writers miss out this inspirational phase is perhaps because it goes against our training, and all our perception of what being an academic is. I was forcibly taught to think in a logical and structured way, and to stop dreaming and reflecting. Yet critical thinking, as used by scientists, social scientists and all the arts disciplines, involves exploration and experimentation. Attempting to stay within the box and only use a small part of our thinking capacity (the logical), cramps and constrains our thinking to the boring. Here is what one writer found liberating:

> Because you can only learn by doing it.
>
> (An academic writer)

This can feel frustrating at first to those who have never experienced it previously. I do, however, find writers take off with these methods, once they've started. Starting writing is the key, rather than just reading and thinking about what I'm saying. Most people these days do experience writing with no pre-thought: texting, tweeting, emailing, blogging, for example. If we think of this as speaking to the other person on the screen, well Phase 1 writing is not so very different. Here is Clare's experience:

> These writing techniques make a channel in the sand with a stick,
>
> Water wells right up from underneath immediately,
>
> Sometimes faster than others.
>
> Like discovery rather than creation.
>
> (Clare Shephard)

A power of *Phase 1 Writing* is that ideas, theories and examples can bud and form under our scribbling fingers, seemingly on their own. Clare says 'Like discovery rather than creation'. Academic writing is always based on a foundation of strong scholarly and original research. We have already created what we are going to write. The actual writing process is one of rediscovering what is already there, and helping it to find its communicable form on the page. It's finding a pointed stick strong enough to channel down through the sand of everyday functional thinking and being, to the clear water of what we already know, have reflected upon and even theorised. This 'rough' writing generally comes out very clearly. Peter Elbow says that he can often understand his students' rough free writing, whereas he frequently can't their carefully revised essays (2012: 97).

Emotion: a powerful resource

Writing and research are emotional processes (Kara, 2013); writing is also personally risk-taking and exposing. Accepting and working with these rather than struggling against them can enhance writing, rather than constantly dragging it back. Even worse than struggling is denying them, working doggedly to put awareness of such vulnerability out of mind.

PhD or doctoral writing, although similar to writing for publication, imposes specific forces often according to rules or instructions not of students' own making, which can engender strong feelings. Writing for publication is emotionally charged because I am working on my own: I am responsible for saying what I want and need to say clearly and fully, and it is up to me to get it published in as widely read and prestigious form as possible. Further than this, my research, and therefore my expression of it, fires me: it's my life's work and I am emotionally involved in it and in its expression.

What do I mean by saying that working with my emotions can enhance my writing? I mean that I can beneficially use my emotions as data. Emotions are a gift to inform humans about how things are for us; we ignore them at our peril. A symptom of leprosy is loss of pain in the skin and below; patients do not experience burning or cutting and so injure themselves seriously: pain is a gift to prevent injury.

We need to make the most of every resource, and emotion is a strong, if frequently overlooked, resource. I feel apprehensive about writing something: this means I need to take particular care, perhaps research the surrounding field in the literature extra thoroughly, or be more vigilant scrutinising my data so I make as few assumptions as possible in my results and discussion sections. I feel elated and want to celebrate because a section has flowed from my fingers to the screen in just the right way (perhaps I'm a writer after all?). Well, can I look back and work out what were the conditions which enabled this best possible of all writing situations, so I can repeat it as often as possible? Feelings, including pain and anxiety are a gift, but a gift which needs attention and awareness. Pat Thomson talks usefully about this in a blog post with responses (Thomson, 2013).

Stephen

I think anger is really important in academic writing. I find much of my writing is a consequence of my feelings 'against' social injustice, ignorance, prejudice and so on. An interesting biography of the philosopher Sartre (who explored his ideas through plays and stories as well as 'academic' writing) was titled *Writing Against* (Hayman, 1986). For Sartre, and I think many writers, anger and similar emotions are the fuel which feeds their writing. The text is the fire which results.

But while anger may often fuel writing, I think it is vital that anger is not *expressed* in academic writing (at least, not normally). To do so would be to confuse the fuel with the fire. Anger needs to be reflected upon, worked through and explored until I can hold myself at a distance from it and then marshal my argument. Often potentially good articles and powerful writing are spoilt because the reader is more struck by the writer's anger than by what the writer is angry about. And it is the object of anger that is important if social injustice, for example, is to be addressed. At its worst, I have felt like suggesting a prospective journal contributor consider visiting a therapist rather than writing academically.

So Gillie's Phase 1 type of writing is really useful for making use of powerful feelings which may be an important motivation for writing but must not overpower it.

Phase 2: Redraft to communicate with your reader

Phase 2 is when I move focus from *what* I have to say, which is what Phase 1 is about, towards *to whom* I wish to address it. I already have a draft to work upon; now I envisage my reader and what they want to know from me, and how to say it appropriately to them. Different readers need to be addressed in different ways. This means choosing and shaping material for this specific reader, modifying and even rejecting certain strands. It also means something more general: ensuring my writing is clear and communicative, positive and coherent for that audience.

Perhaps the Phase 2 focus has been routinely overlooked because academic writers tend to focus on the message to be imparted, rather than standing outside ourselves enough to perceive our readers as specific people. Yet a message not only has to be carefully constructed, it also has to be constructively received, if it is to have any impact. Focusing upon our specific readers can ensure our vital material is understood by them, absorbed into their own research and referred to in their ensuing publications: those precious citations every academic needs.

I've just peer-reviewed a paper which ideally should be accepted with no revision. The content seemed so fascinating, yet at the same time strangely elusive and disconnected from me, the reader. I reread it and realised the author was writing entirely to himself, not to his reader at all. I recommended he redraft with his specific readership in mind, giving the paper a good solid form and structure with a communicative introduction and conclusion.

Phase 3: Edit for posterity to ensure clarity, grammar, correct references ...

Phase 3 is preparing the carefully worked manuscript for publication by paying attention to the way I use language, both for euphony and correctness, to ensure ease and joy of reading. I now turn to studying matters such as the choice of words as well as the particular needs of my publisher (with regard to house style, references, etc.).

This phase often gets skimped or missed out because, although many academic writers get very anxious about grammar, punctuation and so on, they have no idea how to tackle it positively. Many feel it's knowing how to do it right. By 'right' they mean by the book; and yet they don't have the book, don't know where to find it and don't know how to make use of it when they do. There are academic writers who are so focused on getting their research findings or theories out there into the big world they forget that how it is expressed is vitally important. I think many feel: if my message is important enough it will be heard, understood and acted upon (acknowledged and cited), however I write it. This is not so. Much that is potentially useful, in all the disciplines, is rejected by journal editors or read by only a handful because it was impenetrable to its readership, inappropriate to that journal or just plain boring.

Stephen

When I examine a PhD thesis or review proposals for publication I often find that I cannot remember what I have just read, or that I've lost the gist of the argument. My former habitual response was that it must be my fault: I was not concentrating hard enough; or I was not really a very good reader; or I'm not familiar enough with the subject matter. Then it dawned on me that I wasn't at fault, that in academic life one is expected to read text which is, quite simply, badly written.

There seems to be an assumption that what matters are the ideas communicated, not the means of communication. Writing is just a clerical or technical matter whose mastery is unproblematic and a natural accomplishment of any academic: we are ideas people not wordsmiths.

My difficulties with reading articles (both published and for review) is more often the consequence of their being badly written. But what is striking is that well-written articles are invariably reviewed more favourably. A well-written article that has shortcomings is returned with helpful suggestions for revision and resubmission. A badly written one is rejected outright because the reviewer never really grasped what was being communicated.

Most journal referees and PhD examiners – just like most other academics – have no idea the writing process is important. It's the ideas they think they are looking for, not the means by which they are expressed. However, in actual practice, they are invariably impressed by a well-written paper *even though they don't realise it.* I can recall, on several occasions, refereeing a group of papers with a team. On those occasions we would invariably reach a large degree of agreement. While most of my colleagues saw this agreement in terms of the quality of the ideas, I became very aware that the well-received papers were invariably well written.

With this in mind I sometimes think writing is like seduction: the reader is seduced by the text, but unaware of the seduction. The seducer (the author), on the other hand, knows exactly what they are doing. The seducer never loses sight of the person to be seduced.

The reviewer or examiner feeling lost in poor writing is often because the writer loses sight of the reader. That's easy to do when writing: I get absorbed in my own thinking and take my mind off the reader. This is where I find the idea of three phases helpful. I don't usually follow them step by step (although some prefer that), but apply myself to the three different purposes of writing: to clarify for myself; to communicate with my reader; and to contribute to the field of knowledge. When I lose the gist of the text as a reader it is usually because the writer has failed to appreciate all three. And the achievement of the final purpose of academic writing, which is to contribute to the body of knowledge, demands the achievement of the other two.

As a PhD examiner or reviewer of academic journals, once I have committed myself to examine or review a text I am more or less bound to read through to the end. As a 'normal' reader of a book or journal article, however, I can discard the book or article at any stage. Under these circumstances seductive power is even more crucial. Writers failing to maintain my interest lose me for good. A publisher is therefore likely to give the quality of writing an even more prominent place in their criteria for publication.

Readers are interested in what we have to say rather than us writers as people. Academic writing is neither memoir nor polemic; it does not rant. Either of these, or any other personal involvement, in the Phase 1 writing is perfect, because it can be thoroughly expressed and explored, until a draft focused upon the specific interests of a readership can be developed at Phase 2. George Orwell started the whole discussion about Bad Writing in 1946 with essays 'Why I Write' and 'Politics and the English Language'. With his carefully worked on command of language he told his readers:

> One can write nothing readable unless one constantly struggles to efface one's own personality. Good prose is like a window pane.
>
> (Orwell, 1984: 10)

At Phase 2 a strong argument needs to be developed which communicates. Readers do not want to be distracted from the argument by writers' emotion; they want to think of their own feelings in response to the writer's critical argument and discussion. They want to know *why* we feel strongly enough about the subject to write an academic paper. The writer's response to the reader's all important *why* is critical argument, not expression of feeling. Here's my version of an old writers' saying:

> Put your bleeding heart on the page when you first write (Phase 1). Clean off the blood when redrafting (Phase 2), but yet allow the passion to remain in the final draft (Phase 3).

How to Use the Three Phases

Everyone uses the three phases of writing slightly differently. Unlike Stephen I find it helpful to follow the three phases of writing in order, and circle back to revisit earlier phases as necessary. Many wish to extend their enquiry by returning to Phase 1 writing, perhaps feeling their theory or analysis of their data is incomplete, or needing to be reinspired by this dynamic type of writing. Many sensibly return to Phase 2 methods to check that they really are engaging appropriately with the right readers. The material written by re-engaging with an earlier phase will then need to be subjected to either one or both of the later phases, thorough editing, for example (Phase 3).

Working in this way will enable my writing to:

- draw upon the wealth of my experience and knowledge
- communicate well to its intended readership
- give a coherent message/line of argument with good form and structure
- develop this theme persuasively
- have a clear progression, taking readers by the hand from beginning to end
- say what I want it to say, clearly, succinctly, and as far as possible, correctly.

 Don't just read: WRITE!

Here are activities that will help you move from thinking about writing, to actually doing it.

1 Tell in writing the story of an inspiration or insight in your research, an experience relative to the publication you are working on now. It might be recent, or some time ago. Allow yourself to write about the first occasion which comes to mind, or rather to hand. Be as descriptive as you like; it might be useful to remember you have five senses (sight, touch, hearing, smell, taste).

2 Write in response to this question; it might come out as a list, or a single paragraph, or a lengthy piece – write whatever comes:
In what way might the publication you are working on create significant change?

3 Write about your own writing past. How did you write when you were a child? Was it different at school than at home? Think about letters, lists, reports, minutes, exams. If you speak more than one language, how is it different to write in one or the other?

4 Is there anything in your research which makes you feel emotional in any way: angry, upset, hurt, very happy, excited … ? Write this feeling out as fully as you like: use felt tips on a big piece of paper if you like. Remember this is a private expression, for no one else to read but you; though of course it is yours to share if you wish.

And READ some more:

Carnell, E., MacDonald, J., McCallum, B. and Scott, M. (2008). *Passion and Politics: Academics Reflect on Writing for Publication*. London: University of London: Institute of Education.
In this study of academics who are well published, the authors examine seven key themes: the journey to becoming a writer; identities; going about writing; producing a

text; engaging in the process; the politics of writing for publication; and writing, thinking and learning.

Clark, R. and Ivanic, R. (1997) *The Politics of Writing*. London: Routledge.
Although addressed primarily to people who teach writing, this book raises a lot of questions about what lies behind writing and its political significance.

Richardson, L. (1990) *Writing Strategies: Reaching Diverse Audiences*. London: SAGE.
An extremely good writer on the processes of writing, in this essay Richardson discusses, amongst other issues, approaching and successfully addressing diverse audiences.

3

Beginnings

Setting good groundwork makes the business of starting to write hopeful, creative and dynamic. This chapter discusses finding necessary conditions and positive attitudes, and how to find our own writing voices. The 'tin-opener' question stems – *Why, What, How, Who, When, Where* – are then introduced, and their usefulness explained to enable a critical engagement with, and clarity about, the research to be addressed.

Seamus: I know what kind of teacher I am. But what kind of writer am I? Is the way I should write for academics different from the way I write for my students? Why? How?

Helena: My painting is recognisably mine. I know who I am when I paint. Who am I when I write academically? Can there be a 'me' in academic writing? And I hope this chapter will provide me with some very straightforward questions to start me off on the writing. That would be really helpful in unsticking me so I can really start.

Lee: I thought all I needed was to get my English right. Now I learn I need to start from a good place in order to begin to write up my research well and write good academic English.

Joseph: What kind of discourse is academic writing? This 'theory of writing' didn't look much like theory in sociology to me. Perhaps when I see how it's put into practice it will become clear.

Foundations

Where and when we write, and our attitude to it, can really affect the pace and flow of writing, and even what is written. Understanding and working with our own particular needs which feed our creativity can make the difference between satisfying successful writing and frustrating drudgery.

> Academic writing is, in public academic discourse, seen as a straightforward, intellectually-driven and logically-ordered process. Hence, traditionally, where guidance and support on academic writing has existed, the focus has been on technical issues ... Little attention has been paid to the more holistic aspects, such as the lecturer-writer's sense of self and identity, their emotional orientation to their writing and their creative process ... Whilst the main task of academic writing is to *present* intellectual ideas, the *production* of academic writing is not solely an intellectual activity ... The problems experienced by academics in their writing are rarely intellectual ones.
>
> (Antoniou and Moriarty, 2008: 158, 160)

A cycle of work, rest and re-creation is vital; as is developing what kind of writer I've worked out I am. I, for example, am a fidget when starting writing: constantly finding I'm on my feet wandering around while I think. Once I'm steaming ahead I suddenly stop and wonder why I'm so starving hungry and have a numb bum, and realise hours have gone by. If I made myself sit still at the fidgeting stage, it would be very hard and unproductive, just as making myself stop for set meal times when I'm in the flow would mean I'd lose unreplaceable stuff.

At a certain stage of drafting and redrafting I also need to scribble on paper with a pencil in bed or outside. A successful novelist I once met starts writing as soon as she wakes up: in bed, in her nightclothes; she is very fierce if any of her family attempt to interrupt her creative period (this was also poet W.H. Auden's method). Another novelist friend writes in the morning, goes for a walk after lunch, then returns to redrafting, or other non-first-draft jobs.

> I discovered how much I enjoyed writing by hand.
>
> (Academic writing course member)

Effective expression is affected by so many things, some of them seemingly tiny. Some people write well in the morning but not the afternoon, some better in summer than winter. Some have bursts for weeks and then nothing (that's me); sometimes the computer might be good to write on, sometimes very much not, and a pencil is needed. Some respond well to making a clear plan and sticking to it as far as possible; to others this would spell death to the organic nature of their thinking and writing.

An initial go at writing sometimes doesn't feel good, if this happens it's worth trying a different place and/or time, and/or different materials. Pencil and paper create different results to computers; black fountain pen on thick new paper different from blue biro on second-hand scraps, and different again from a thick red felt tip on flip-chart paper. Using a different font, such as a handwriting one, can be surprisingly conducive and worth trying. Where we write can significantly affect the product we create. It might not always be the same place. Cally Guerin (Aitchison et al., 2013) writes most often in her kitchen, despite having a study at home.

Some find it useful to think through ideas absolutely anywhere, and perhaps do Phase 1 writing in bed or by a lake, by the sea or a river, in a café or library, on a hilltop. Others find it helpful to preface a writing session with a non-writing reflective period, such as thinking through ideas on a long car or train journey. Reflecting while walking is an age-old writers' habit. Wordsworth and Coleridge famously clambered over many of the highest English Lake District peaks in their pursuit of peaceful, yet physically active reflective space in a beautiful place.

'Shut up and Write' sessions, which started in San Francisco Bay area with creative writers have spread worldwide to PhD students, and academics. They have one contact point which advertises meetings at regular, prearranged times in places such as cafés, when they have periods of silently writing or working which are short, such as twenty-five minutes of focused concentration (pomodoro technique) with convivial breaks (O'Donnell, 2011; Mewburn, 2011). Such sessions are, it seems, brilliant for preventing some writers from wasting time; they'd be useless to me as I'd be paralysed by others being near me; I know a couple, both novelists, who cannot even write in the same house: he has a garden writing shed.

When we write – in the middle of the night, early morning hours – can make a difference too. Short accessible times for writing can be really conducive; writing whenever there is time available, even if brief. This is not only my experience, and of many people I've worked with, but is also the finding of research. Robert Boice (e.g. 1997) and Stephen Krashen (2002) found that this is the pattern of successful writers who write a lot. Since this is a tip from experienced writers it's worth a try, however hard it is to believe when starting out.

Some of these elements might seem insignificant until they are changed, and the benefit experienced. Suggesting personal preferences for how and where to write academically might seem odd: surely I sit at my desk and write? Well, that would be the case if we were machines who could churn out a succinct, flowing, readable output from our mass of research data. Each individual writer will find their own idiosyncrasies. This writing is ours to experiment with.

I've also learned from my work with helping critically ill or dying people to write what they need to before it's too late (Bolton, 1999, 2011). They do not have the time to worry about how they are perceived, to feel exposed or be anxious about being bad at writing. They have things to say to the living in very limited time, and they get on with it. And they invariably write it extremely well (frequently heartbreakingly so).

Writing can be conjured when there is space for it; it just needs a decision to start. Waiting for magical readiness is a futile time-waster: we conjure readiness to write when we need it, not when it needs it. Part of the problem for the inexperienced and anxious is waiting for some sort of permission to see ourselves as 'writers'. Writing works when we write, write and write some more. It works when I write what I knew I wanted to say, what I didn't want to say and what I didn't know I wanted to say. It works when I tell the story in full, realising I can edit out bits later, or take out bits which belong somewhere else. Ideas can be tried out and rejected, experimented with, improved upon. Jane found this process opened up so much more in her research:

> I thought I'd worked through everything possible, until I began to write in this way.
>
> (Jane)

Writing, academic just like any other, involves the whole of the writer's being. As Hélène Cixous (1995) told us, we write with our bodies, not just our minds. Our hands, whether holding a pen or tapping a keyboard, create words; I have often written with intensity – with a burning nib and boiling ink – and then stopped to reread and mutter: where on earth did all that come from? We write with our intellectual, physical, emotional, spiritual, social and cultural selves. Questions are relevant such as: Why do I want to write? Who am I? What am I so passionate about that I want to spend lifeblood and valuable hours writing about it? What are my values that this writing explores and expresses? Where do I want this writing to take me? Who do I want to listen to me? Why? When and how do I want to write? Here is Bernadette Knewstubb about a strategy she uses to get herself to write.

27

Writing a Rant!

If I leave writing about part of my research until I have worked it all through, the problem has become too big, and so I don't write anything. So instead I write a rant. I get down my frustration with a situation, research position or policy. This is usually written in the first-person with lots of damning language such as 'researchers fail to see', 'vastly demanding', 'suffer', 'lack of insight' – these terms may refer to researchers, academics, university management or government agendas.

The process of turning a rant into a piece of academic prose takes me some time, but there are a number of process steps I take to get me under way

1   Remove emotive adjectives or adverbs such as 'vastly'

2   Turn negative reflections on research to date in to positives (with limitations), e.g. Smith shows us that ... but this needs to be extended to allow for ...

3   If I'm still struggling, try to remove myself by using passive rather than active verbs: 'I believe' becomes 'It might be argued that'

Once those discourse elements have been adjusted, I can stand back a little from and review the text more coolly – where are the gaps in my argument? Have I represented the literature fairly? What do I think should be done about it? Should I do some more research to find a solution, rather than just seeing the problem? Is what I'm saying really a new contribution, or has someone else already said it? I can't always do this with my thinking, or even in verbal discussions, but when faced with a bland printed text, with little emotive language, I can start to treat my thinking in a more academic way.

(Bernadette Knewstubb)

Seasoned writers have worked out strategies for dealing with their inner terrorist who tells them there's no point sitting down to write today because they are useless (for some of their tips, see Chapter 8). They know, for example, that if writing sessions are put off and put off until the perfect occasion arises then that terrorist will take serious and triumphant hold. Whereas satisfaction is gained from having written even just a paragraph in a grabbed fifteen minutes: a start has been made. Making realistic use of modest clearings of time and space keeps up the flow and the energy steady. The ancient Greeks knew that the methodical steady tortoise wins over the racy hare.

Experienced writers also know that waiting to be in the *right mood* is only a delaying tactic. Writing is work: if doctors and builders waited until they were in the right frame of mind, everyone would suffer.

With a strategy of writing frequently, even if sometimes for short bursts, writing continues in our minds while we are doing all sorts of other things, such as travelling to work or eating alone. It can come to the foreground in sometimes surprising ways, offering original ideas or solutions. I have often woken in the night, spent half an hour tussling with a seemingly intractable issue, solved it and been immensely glad in the morning when I sit at my desk again. The novelist R.L. Stevenson, author of *Treasure Island* (2012 [1883]) and *Dr Jekyll and Mr Hyde* (2002 [1886]), went so far as to plan for writing problems to be solved at night: he said he gave them to his 'brownies' to solve (these are little helpful people like elves or fairies). Becoming abstracted, or even suddenly saying seemingly irrelevant things during a meal time or other social occasion can make the company of anyone involved in a long writing project exasperating to non-writers. I'm lucky I suppose in sharing my life with another academic writer; though Stephen sometimes finds it trying when I'm writing poetry as my mind might leap to anything at all.

Stephen

I'm sure we all write – and think – very differently. Gillie's mind does indeed leap at anything at all and she is naturally inclined to a more poetic way of thinking and writing. In contrast, I tend to think in a more logical or scientific manner. I can become obsessive in my struggle to pursue a line of argument with things sometimes remaining unresolved until I have an occasional flash of insight. At the risk of being simplistic, one might say that I am a more structured thinker and she a more creative one.

If something like that is so, it is interesting that I have less need to follow through the phases of writing as a procedure or sequence of activities, vital though the concept of phases is here. It is as though the structure of phases that Gillie develops in this book is a useful conceptual device for me, helping me to identify those aspects of my writing that I need to work on. But for Gillie it also provides a structured procedure. Readers of this book may be more like me or like Gillie (or different from both of us). There is no right way to be.

Sometimes my choice of how to write something has been really striking. I remember once, I was struggling to write the fine details of a difficult group discussion. I couldn't remember *exactly* what had been said and, of course, I didn't know what individuals had been thinking and feeling in this emotionally intense discussion. But I had a very strong impression and sense of what had taken place. It then suddenly occurred to me that I could write down what had been said and thought as if I really did have access to people's thoughts. Thus my written account soon became a fiction – albeit a fiction which represented what I thought had taken place. I then subjected this fiction to the kind of interpretive analysis that would have been appropriate in a purely factual account.

I later sent each group member my account of the events together with my interpretation. Several responded with astonishment about the plausibility of my account of people's thoughts and feelings and there was much further discussion based on this. Realising that this 'fictional' way of writing seemed to have some value I presented my report and the fictional account (together with an explanation of why I wrote fictionally) to the *British Educational Research Journal*. It appeared that there was considerable disagreement between referees about whether a work of 'fiction' could be published in a high-ranking social science research journal. But eventually this was published (Rowland, 1991). Since then, many research studies using fictional writing in the exploration of social phenomena have been published.

Now I'm not recommending here that if you have forgotten the actual results of a chemistry experiment you should just fictionalise the data and expect to publish it. What the circumstances might be for a fictional presentation of results or ideas to be accepted is beyond the scope of this book. But it became clear that the way research is written may have all sorts of methodological implications. My initial foray into writing fiction as a part of my research taught me two things:

1   An innovative way of writing may help in understanding a problem;
2   Different ways of writing may be appropriate to different research methodologies (or in different disciplines) and acceptable to high-ranking journals.

Imagine how a drama critic's review of a play might be written using the language normally appropriate in a chemistry experiment, and you will see what I mean.

I am left with this interesting query: to what extent does my research methodology constrain (or enable) the possibility of different voices to tell the story of my research?

What Kind of Writer am I? What Kind do I Want to be?

We all do have a choice as to what kind of writers we are: it is not laid down by some academic authority. I am my own academic authority, to an extent ('author' and 'authority' come from the same etymological root). And I can write in different ways on different occasions, for different publications and readers.

When I started writing I was far too enthusiastic, and wanted to persuade everyone of the incredible value of my research. In my academic writing I had to learn to 'hedge' my claims (see Gillett, 2013). First-draft sentences had to be changed from such as 'reflective writing enables professionals to …', to 'reflective writing can enable … .', or 'may enable', or 'might'. I had to learn to use 'likely', 'often', 'possible'. I still write first drafts overenthusiastically. But tempering my claims to what my data actually showed gave a realistic picture of my findings because my research, as is anyone's, was necessarily limited in scope. I have never felt that limitation, but had to learn to express it in my writing. I had to develop a narrator for my academic writing who was much cooler, calmer and logical than me, who was less enthusiastic than the narrator of my professional publications, and far more tempered than the narrator of my popular publications (see pp. 114, 134–5 for more on the 'narrator').

Here is a strategy for finding our own writing preferences. I have used it with a huge numbers of writers over the years, and it never fails to illuminate. It is to undertake a critical reading of self-chosen publications by successful authors in a range of genres. First we find a piece of writing (academic, novel, poetry, short story, journalism, biography, etc.: ANYTHING) we've admired at any time of our lives. Then pick a remembered small section, and reread it to remind ourselves why we liked it.

Is this how I would like to write? Look carefully at this text: is it concise and punchy, loose and discursive, full of dialogue, succinct and lyrical? All writing has a style; academic writing is no different. Every single writer develops a distinctive voice, even those who are just trying to be as academic and intellectual as possible.

One group of writers who did this exercise brought a fascinatingly diverse range of publications. I didn't keep a note of what they all were, but here is the list of what each member deduced from the texts they brought, about how they would like to write:

- Meditative, reflective, descriptive, clearly written
- Off-beat humour, challenging
- Gentle, but memorable, gets to you underneath
- Economical
- Powerful, thought-provoking
- Easy to read, short sentences, short paragraphs, the readers don't get lost but yet it arouses emotions: things that get me
- Evocative, visual images, atmospheric, concise
- Mastery of subject matter, making a dry subject matter witty and simple, also critical, elegant and non-aggressive
- Well-constructed, plot with surprise, works on many levels, imaginative, craftsmanship, every word counts, beauty and art are not sinful

Each reader here has looked beyond the content of each publication to the way the writer has constructed the extract. Here are some questions we could ask of the text:

- How has the author made a complex idea clear and seem straightforward?
- What is particular about this writing to its field? Is it different from how it would be structured in your field?

- How did the author structure the paragraphs, how did it start and end?
- How are the paragraphs connected to previous and following ones?
- What are the sentences like? Passive or active? Concise and clear?

Stephen and I would like to present a passage each of our own choosing, to show what writing we like and admire, and how reflecting upon it makes us think we'd like to write. My choice is a well-known text, from *Emma* by Jane Austen.

> 'Every friend of Miss Taylor must be glad to have her so happily married.' [said Mr Knightley]
>
> 'And you have forgotten one matter of joy to me,' said Emma, 'and a very considerable one – that I made the match myself. I made the match you know, four years ago; and to have it take place, and be proved in the right, when so many people said Mr Weston would never marry again, may comfort me for anything.'
>
> Mr Knightley shook his head at her. Her father fondly replied, 'Ah! my dear, I wish you would not make matches and foretell things, for whatever you say always comes to pass. Pray do not make any more matches.'
>
> 'I promise you to make none for myself, papa; but I must, indeed, for other people. It is the greatest amusement in the world! ... '
>
> 'I do not understand what you mean by "success,"' said Mr Knightley. 'Success supposes endeavour ... Where is your merit? What are you proud of? You made a lucky guess; and *that* is all that can be said.'
>
> (Austen, 1922 [1815]: 7–8)

This extract is very near the beginning of the novel, which has been one of my favourites since I was a young teenager, despite Jane Austen's assertion that she was 'going to take a heroine whom no one but myself will much like' (1922 [1815]: iii). Here, the major characters are before us; they not only tell us all we need to know about their characteristics in these few utterances, they also give us the main thread of the plot. Emma (written through the years of the Napoleonic wars) is impetuous and arrogantly confident of her own powers in her little world; her father, who doesn't like change of any kind, indulgently believes her to be as infallible as she does herself; Mr Knightley does not. Mr Knightley is seen to be kind but firmly practical; his role is to try to keep Emma within ladylike bounds while being honourable and respectful of everyone's feelings and station in life. Emma's misjudged matchmaking, and lack of care about her own future is the novel's plot. We are given all this in these few words. Yet, at the same time as giving this dense information, this brief dialogue sparkles with wit and intrigue. Listen to this view, however, from a respected US author, writing in his journal:

> I am at a loss to understand why people hold Miss Austen's novels at so high a rate, which seem to me vulgar in tone, sterile in artistic invention, imprisoned in the wretched conventions of English society, without genius, wit, or knowledge of the world. Never was life so pinched and narrow. The one problem in the mind of the writer ... is marriageableness ... Suicide is more respectable.
>
> (Ralph Waldo Emerson, 1861, quoted in Henderson and Bernard, 1998: 22)

Reading and reflecting upon this brief passage made me realise I would like to write concisely, with crystal clarity, and with wit and energy.

Stephen

Gillie has asked me to present a passage from a book, to show what kind of writing I admire, but I find that difficult. I have no trouble finding a book I like. The problem is to illustrate what I like about it with a passage. The book – *Gödel, Escher, Bach: An Eternal Golden Braid*, by Douglas Hofstadter (1979) – is subtitled 'A metaphorical fugue on minds and machines in the spirit of Lewis Carroll'. From this title and subtitle this is clearly going to be a pretty complicated book. It is.

In over 700 pages (and I still haven't got to the last one yet) Hofstadter explores the difficult nature of logic and number theory by interweaving discussions and examples from Bach; instances of Escher's drawings of impossible objects and scenes; comic dialogues between Achilles and the tortoise; and equations of formal logic. I couldn't possibly explain in a few sentences what this book aims to achieve. All I need say is that it's pretty damned difficult for someone who is not a mathematician or logician.

What I like about it is the author's playfulness, inventiveness and concern for form and how he uses these to communicate such difficult ideas. Logic and number theory are normally addressed in serious tones with long faces, as if to appeal only to the mathematical nerd. By drawing upon different disciplines of thought Hofstadter presents new ideas in ways that encourage us to make leaps of imagination. Mathematical and scientific understanding demand at least as much of these qualities as do the arts, to my way of thinking.

Research deals with difficult matters and for me (and for most children, I believe) playfulness can open the door to new and original ways of thinking and combinations of ideas. Research also involves invention (for any discovery is also partly invention). The question of whether a theory of numbers is 'invented' or 'discovered' is itself a subject of the philosophy of mathematics. In my research in the social sciences, invention plays a large part. And a concern for form is, for me, key to academic writing. Like musical (or artistic or literary) composition, academic writing is an art. It must therefore be concerned with form. In *Gödel, Escher, Bach* the form of the book, with its interweaving of ideas and approaches, reflects the imaginative interplay(fulness) of ideas in logical and mathematical thinking. I don't believe logical thinkers just think in straight lines.

What I would like to achieve in academic writing is to gain insights, and present them to my readers, in ways that reflect a width of experience and variety of intellectual and emotional responses.

Using the Tin Openers: Why, What, How, Who, When, Where

These sentence stems are 'tin openers' because, wielded wisely and critically, these six will prise open any subject for us. Five of them help us ask mostly practical questions; the sixth, 'why', asks the intellectual critical questions. These sentence stems will open up any practical, methodological or enquiry issue, especially if allied to the three phases of academic writing introduced in Chapter 1. These phases are:

1 Write for yourself to find out what you know, think, feel, and want to say.
2 Redraft to communicate with your reader.
3 Edit for posterity to offer clarity, clear language, structure, grammar, correct references ...

The strategies and methods appropriate to each of these three phases help to answer these 'tin openers':

- What do I want to communicate?
- Why do I want anyone to hear this?
- How do I want to write it?
- When can I do it?
- With whom might I want to write and how might we collaborate?
- Who can advise and help me?

- Why does anyone want to hear it?
- With whom do I want to communicate?
- How might the paper/thesis/book be focused appropriately for this reader?

- How can I improve it to make it sparkle and shine?
- When should it be published for maximum effect?
- How might I ensure acceptance for publication?

- Where is the best place to publish?
- Where is the best place to write it?

These are my suggestions for useful questions; there are probably many more, some specific to each particular study. Or the questions in these forms might not be quite right and would be better adapted for each individual writer. A dynamic start has been made. In the next chapter we can turn to a specific strategy which will open writing up further, and keep it going forward.

 Don't just read: WRITE!

Here are activities that will help you move from thinking about writing, to actually doing it.

1 How would you like to write?
   Think of a published piece of writing (of any sort) you have appreciated (in whatever way). Reread a typical passage from it. Analyse what it is about it you like: make a list. We would ideally like to write in a similar way to the things we enjoy reading. So you can think of the items on your list as advice to yourself (see above for examples and more about this exercise).
2 Write a 'rant' about your research, then turn it into communicative academic prose (see above for a graphic example).
3 Write a list of questions to yourself about the writing you are working on, each beginning with one of the tin openers (Why, What, How, Who, When, Where), writing a couple of sentences in response to each (see above for a list of sample questions).
4 Respond to these:

   - Where do I write? Where else might I write, to see if it makes any difference (think broadly and imaginatively)?
   - When do I write? When else might I write, to see if it makes any difference?
   - For whom do I write? Do I write to different readers at different times? Think carefully about this one.
   - What do I write with? Could I write with different materials?
   - How do I write? Do I take care of myself as I write? Do I push or force myself, or let myself off the hook too often?
   - Why do I write? The million dollar question …

5 You have an important message to impart. Imagine there is no one out there listening and you are getting very frustrated. Shout onto the paper what it is you wish them to hear. You could even use coloured felt tips on A1 paper if you thought that might help your writing to shout louder.

And READ some more:

Belcher, W. (2009) *Writing your Journal Article in Twelve Weeks: A Guide to Academic Publishing Success.* Thousand Oaks, CA: SAGE.
Written from long experience of teaching writers of scholarly papers in social science and the humanities, this guide has very useful elements. It would also be helpful for an academic writers' group.

Crasswell, G. and Poore, M. (2012) *Writing for Academic Success*, 2nd edn. London: SAGE.
This useful guide includes much about ways to write and publish online and about cross-cultural and interdisciplinary practices.

Goodson, P. (2013) *Becoming an Academic Writer: Fifty Exercises for Paced, Productive and Powerful Writing.* London: SAGE.
A useful and thorough text.

Phase 1: Write for Myself

4

Explore, Experiment, Find Out

The key to starting inspirational writing is to write. And then write some more. This chapter introduces an unfailingly effective strategy which is straightforward and enjoyable. How to reread writing, possibly sharing it with others, and keeping a research journal are also covered.

Seamus: Where do I start? I like the idea of experiment and exploration. That's how I often approach new ideas with my students. Perhaps I need to play a bit with writing. But how?

Helena: Well, in design we use all sorts of techniques to help find out what we want to express and how and why (see, I'm using the tin-opener questions!). So perhaps a good way of starting to write might be NOT to focus yet, but allow myself to write the equivalent of a sketchbook, storyboard and mood-board. Phew that would be a relief.

And then perhaps I can share and discuss it all with others. Perhaps I could continue doing that throughout all the writing phases and stages. Is this where a reflective research journal comes in? I could keep notes of where I've got to and all my thoughts and feelings?

Lee: I'm beginning to struggle. I nearly stopped reading when Gillie wrote about that novel. But I can see what Stephen meant about the interesting form of his chosen book, I think. I need help with my discussion section. I must express what I think is essential about my research. I've never done this before. It has always been done by another member of the team.

(Continued)

(Continued)

Joseph: I always write what I want to say, but then I find when I submit a paper it gets rejected and the reviewers often miss the whole point of what I'm getting at. I hope this chapter shows me how to see if my ideas are understandable to others before I get to the stage of submission.

Starting Out

Experienced writers write an awful lot more words than they publish, bearing in mind that the waste paper basket (or delete button, or command to open a new file and abandon the old) is the writer's best friend. Words are expendable. We might initially use far more detail than necessary, for example, or too much from the raw data. At the time this enabled a full exploration of the issues and elements. Later these could be pared down straightforwardly. This process is far from a waste of time, as greater understanding of the issues has been constructively gained.

We learn to write by writing. Intending every written word to be destined for publication is a route to failure. The effective writing process is one of exploration and experimentation, of trying out and then trying again, and then again. And then the subject of research can seem to open out, as the poet Robert Frost found with his writing:

> The delight is in the surprise of remembering something I didn't know I knew ... Step by step the wonder of unexpected supply keeps growing.

(Frost, 1972: 440–1)

The strategy described in this chapter is straightforward: it enables me to engage fully with the 'tin-opener' questions introduced in Chapter 3. It is to explore what I know, understand, think and feel about subjects I tackle, as fully and in depth as possible. This sort of writing could be thought of as initial exploratory notes, which might not read like academic writing yet. This germinal stage, which need never be read by anyone else, focuses wholly on the content of what needs to be said, experimenting with and exploring ideas, theories, descriptions and connections. Through this process the writer also finds and learns to use their own individual writing voice confidently and clearly. Redrafting this explorative writing for the appropriate academic readership belongs to the second phase. Here is a writing course member's initial reaction to this:

I am interested in all this and somewhat relieved but also a little disbelieving:

- Surely academic writing is not supposed to be understandable

- Surely I am not allowed to be intuitive

- Most of all, surely no one will want to hear what I want to say in a way that makes sense to me.

So, like learning a new language, writing appears to be more about having the confidence to get started, keep going, and the courage to give it to someone else to read.

One issue is understandability. It seems that dense, incoherent language is the order of the day in many academic publications. There is a sort of upman(person)-ship in many big (need a dictionary/thesaurus to understand) words being used. Also points are awarded for very long sentences that take sharp turns, meander a bit longer and then arrive somewhere but nowhere.

A little like that last sentence!

(Academic writing course member)

Many authorities strongly advocate beginning with a plan, rather than the Phase 1 type writing recommended in this chapter. There may well be some focused narrow-range projects which would benefit from being kept on the rails thus. Phase 1, 2 and 3 type writing is advocated by Stephen and I as it can lead to writing which is inspirational to write and inspirational to read. And here are some positive reactions to these methods:

I appreciated learning how to start writing without being so stressful of the content and organisation, and let my writing flow with very interesting results.

I'm left with a surprisingly 'light' mind, with lots of room for new thinking and creativity. This *is* a surprise – not expected, but really exciting.

It's tiring actually, which surprised me.

(Academic writing course members)

This chapter explains fully how to do Phase 1 writing, and then how to work on it towards more focused writing. It concludes with advice on developing appropriate and constructive attitudes to writing, by engaging in Phase 1 type of writing regularly: this could be called a personal research journal.

Write to Learn

> The free writing was always helpful; it enabled fresh problems to emerge, that I addressed in further free writing.
>
> Writing freely without structure was a great thing to learn. It seemed natural, although I had never done it before. It made writing the points clearly and easily without being limited with the structure.
>
> (Academic writing course member)

Here's how this first explorative stage of writing works. Good news about this method is that it doesn't need very much time to come up with results.

Free write for at least *six minutes* before settling down to write properly. I write whatever comes into my mind in whatever order, even if it's totally non-academic. This can identify the doors that need closing in my mind (see Chapter 1), perhaps by listing pressing concerns which I can return to later, or working out what I am anxious about. I can then create a time-slot later in the day for safely opening that door and letting the mayhem of personal issues out when I have time and patience to deal with them. This method also gets words going in a really straightforward way. The blank page or screen is the most scary thing to any writer. So even if none of these words is valuable for the current project, the mind has begun to limber up for writing and words are coming out. AND – sometimes – startlingly valuable inspirations occur during this initial write.

> Initial writing – 6 minute 'dump'
>
> At the moment I feel the urge to pee. But I can't go because I've gone already and people might look at me funny. I am also very hungry and wondering when we might eat, and also what we will eat.
>
> Like learning a new language, writing appears to be more about having the confidence to get started, keep going, and the courage to give it to someone else to read.
>
> Which brings me to my next point – the importance of being in the correct place for myself, with people who 'get me', what I am doing and where I come from.
>
> Perhaps the issues about the difficulty of collaboration is that people do not (usually) come from the same place, but almost defensively actually work hard at coming from different places often not to improve the writing, but rather to put their point of view across rather than yours.
>
> (Anon)

In this most basic initial writing method, the *Six Minute Write*, words determine where they want to go. Reading them afterwards, I find out what I've said, and quite often what I think, believe, understand, know. This follow-the-flow-of-my-mind, key to all writing, is the secret to mining some of the riches of the mind, which can otherwise get overlooked. I think about it a great deal during the whole writing process, but have to write it otherwise it slips out of my consciousness again. Every writer needs to explore and experiment with the kind of writer they are, making as few as possible prior assumptions about themselves and their abilities and requirements.

For this very first stage writing we invent our own rules; it is ours to do what we want. Nobody else is going to see it unless I decide they may, so it's OK if it only makes sense to me. If I want someone else to read it, I can redraft, cut out or alter later. Here is one experienced writer's reflection on free writing:

> Two middle-aged women walk unsteadily on the pebbles towards the waves. Gulls have scattered the rubbish around, hunting for plunder. The two women wade deeper and deeper until they're both striking out, swimming in the morning, their heads above the waves. Learn from that. The words come how and when they choose, and only then can I shape them. I want to honour that mystery, that sense of my writing making its own rules, and I the servant of those lines. I need to honour the silences too: they have their place. Words help me make sense of the brambles where I try to carve a path.
>
> (Robert Hamberger)

Writing out half-formed thoughts and plans helps find out what I think, and what I still need to discover. It is for myself only; this way I can grasp the slippery beginnings of ideas and not worry if they appear muddled: I know the time for sorting them out is not yet. They *need* to be unconstrained initially; a researcher risks limiting their research by overdetermining their findings. Whether the publication presents clinical quantitative data or reports an action research study, important lines of argument and logical narrative sequence often emerge from what might initially seem confusion.

Such writing requires courage, but then writing does anyway. This is a strategy which can help us think through what we want to say, know, think and feel. Here are the thoughts of three writers new to free writing:

> 6 minutes gives me a transcendent space; peaceful; helpful to think I can return there any time.
>
> I found I really enjoyed free writing for 6 minutes. It was very useful just to clear my thoughts, develop ideas, or even just to dump.

I think the 6 minutes free writing is a place to go; I want to get familiar with it so I can go there to stretch my ideas. I have always wondered where people get their stated ideas from. And this is the place for me where I can anchor my ideas. It's also a place where they can be born and nurtured.

(Academic writing course members)

And it can be very helpful to reread this writing fairly quickly. A symptom of early-stage writer's block is feeling a strong emotion against rereading writing. It is well worth struggling against this inhibition. Though some just don't realise how important it is:

It surprised me that I never realised I never read my writing back immediately. I found it so beneficial when I did.

(Academic writing course member)

Stephen

Perhaps my most significant impression from thirty years of refereeing academic papers is that it is really pretty boring. I don't usually like to admit that because I also believe it is very important. A referee has the powerful role of 'gatekeeper' to knowledge, letting some in, shutting others out, not to be taken lightly.

The role of thesis examiner is even more important: a career can hang upon it. Although reading a thesis can be exciting, I have felt it to be at times a boring duty. Because theses are much longer than academic papers, the author really needs to engage the reader.

The texts which keep away the boredom and remind me of my importance as examiner or referee are those where I am convinced the writer learnt from the process of shaping their ideas. This is communicated in the vibrancy of their voice, and cannot be faked. Reading such writing I feel I am playing a part in someone else's discoveries. That really is powerful: the antipathy of boredom.

In my experience, the early phase – whether a *six minute* splurge or a more extended but nevertheless immediate writing – is often when I become aware that I am learning something. It is here that new patterns emerge, new connections are made and I realise that I am on to something. The inevitable sense of excitement, urgency and life of such learning, often born in the early stages of writing, is like the soul of the text, to be reshaped and refined to emerge eventually as the fully fledged paper.

I think it is this vibrancy that affects me as referee or examiner. Then I am hooked, and I will immediately be favourably disposed towards the paper's eventual acceptance, or the thesis being passed.

How to Start

Here is a strategy for beginning each writing session with a constructively open, enquiring and adventurous attitude. It involves a very brief (six minutes) free-flow write, followed by more focused writing. Beginning every writing period with the *six minutes dump* writing generally facilitates greater depth and width, or greater insight into the theories and material under current consideration.

- Take whatever materials feel good for today; this might be very different one time from another.
- Choose where to sit, the most attractive place at the time: under a tree, at the kitchen table, somewhere miles from home or office, or of course at that academic desk, with your tea/coffee beside you and the phone and mobile switched OFF.
- Choose also a peaceful time with at least twenty minutes UNINTERRUPTED, and ALONE.
- Settle comfortably.
- Write on a new sheet of paper or screen (preferably the former).
- Allow thoughts and ideas to settle into a still pool of silence, with no specific subject. Ignore all outside noises/sights/smells. Jot *anything* which occurs to the hand or fingers to put on the page or screen; try to be open – apposite thoughts will arrive next to irrelevant ones. No one need see these notes, and you don't yet know what will lead to what. Allow the writing to write itself for at least six minutes WITHOUT STOPPING, without rereading, and as far as possible without thinking about it. Try not to sit and think AT ALL before beginning: put the pen or pencil on the paper and start writing, in mid-sentence if necessary: allow the hand on the paper to do the initial thinking.
- Our minds hop around, so well might this writing. Allow the words to fall onto the paper, particularly not trying to coerce them into anything academic; the more non-academic stuff which is dumped on the page at this stage, the freer the mind will be to focus in a few minutes' time. What is written in this six minutes might be descriptions; shopping lists, moans about traffic, weather, children, colleagues; an account of something that happened; last night's dream; work or dinner plans: a startling solution to your theory problem; it doesn't matter what it is. Don't stop to question anything: write without thinking.
- We don't think in sentences or logical sequences, so neither might this writing. Only include punctuation, correct grammar and spelling which occurs naturally. FOLLOW the FLOW for six minutes.
- If it gets stuck, just rewrite the last sentence, or look up and describe the surroundings.
- Do this without stopping for six minutes. Write whatever is in your mind. Allow anything to come in any form – scurrilous, moaning, disparate ideas – odd phrases, half sentences, lists – anything. Remember no one else need read it.

- Whatever we write will be right for now, even if it seems to be merely a list of the rubbish and worries at the top of the mind. If what comes is useful to the current project, and it quite often is, we might want to change things later, perhaps remembering better or having rethought. Or the spelling punctuation and grammar might be far from perfect. None of these things matter for now; what matters is letting out now what I think, feel, know, remember, wonder, believe. With this kind of open approach it's impossible to think of such explorative expression as essentially wrong.

After the six minutes is up, without pausing much, and without rereading the *six minutes dump* yet, begin some more focused follow-up writing. This might be continuing from where the writing was left at the previous writing session, or a new subject which has been thought of beforehand. If there is no obvious writing theme, posing a query about the subject of the current writing, by using one of the tin openers (see p. 34), can lead to really useful material.

- Begin to write about your subject, but allow the thoughts to appear on the paper in whatever order (or seeming disorder) they want, similar to the *six-minute writing approach*. Allow your hand(s) to write unhindered by your interfering brain. Do this for fifteen minutes.
- Carry on writing in whatever way seems right, until your hand aches too much to continue.
- Reread and reflect: note down your reflections.
- *Now* you can begin to organise your writing. If you feel the *six minutes dump* hasn't really worked on this occasion, put it on one side and try again another day: our minds don't work to order. Reread all the writing from both days (the first is probably a great deal more useful – inspirational even – than you'd feared).
- This way of beginning to write can be used for any type of writing: reports, academic papers, professional articles, poetry ...
- Using this way of writing, keep notes all through the writing process: of your research, aspects of work you'd like to communicate to others. Writing in the above way, allowing yourself to write whatever comes, will capture vital facts, observations, inspirations, images, thoughts, ideas ...
- Include things colleagues/patients say (dialogues even); notes from readings or other texts (think widely); accounts, stories of experience from now or the past, yours or recounted ones of others.
- Listen; peel all six senses. Ideas will come from odd sources – inside or out.

Six minutes writing

This weekend we are going to Queensberry in Central Otago for two days of sunshine and gardening. We will check on the lettuces and tomatoes hoping that there hasn't been a late frost. Last year the tomatoes were almost ruined by a severe frost in November, but managed to revive themselves from small remaining shoots. They produced many large, delicious tomatoes much to our surprise. My peonies are all up, but I suspect that they won't flower because I shifted them recently. Peonies can be very sulky and temperamental.

(Tracy Rohan)

Two sets of six minute free-flow writing

Right now I have been asked to write, to create, to learn. This process of writing down is contrary to how I have written before because of my need to prove, deliver, excite, justify, and this is why I become stuck. I get stuck because this is another system, like another solar system of thoughts that give greater expression. Another question I raise, is this new system opening my brain power, reactivating my neurons or is it just relaxing and letting myself construct? There you are!!! Asking questions and using words and constructs I am familiar with and who knows what I am missing out on by rethinking these old concepts. Maybe I need to toss them out.

I am starting another six minutes writing, six years later, about where I have progressed in my writing. I have discovered it is an 'initiation period' and the results are something fundamental, even if I have to mould the meanings and statements further. It is a way for me to hear what I have to say and move beyond the circular.

We talk about stepping stones, but these moments were like walking through a river with rolling stones under foot and eventually I would feel my feet, my strength and balance to carry on. I often think about how meditation is described; as a deepening of thoughts, as a stone dropping and eventually effortless and pleasurable. I really want this to happen with my writing, editing and rewriting.

(Lynley Deaker)

Why SIX minutes flow-of-the-mind writing? I can't remember, as I began many years ago. Five was too short and seven not right somehow. Six minutes is one-tenth of an hour, and ten the natural human numerical base (the word digit means both number, and finger or toe). Three more lots of six minutes would be a twenty-four-minute write: a good normal concentration length.

One of the secrets of writing is to keep doing it even when there seems to be nothing there, because:

- writing, just as life, offers a muddle of the good, the bad and the boring: it might seem dull one minute, and full of vitality and significance the next;
- things hold different meanings at different times: a piece of writing might seem irrelevant or nondescript one day: but prove insightful later.

Rereading and Possibly Sharing the Writing

Rereading the *six minute dump*, as well as the more focused writing, can be very useful as these words were written at speed and relatively thought-lessly, so it may contain surprisingly valuable elements. It can then be redrafted or edited, of course. Its contents might be entirely memorable, or, as it is a relatively painless way of helping words appear on the page or screen, they might seem not sufficiently useful to reread. This initial *six minute dump* scribble can be left unread, if that feels right.

What's next? More writing on another day of course. When involved in creating Phase 1 writing, it is most helpful to feel it is private and not to be shared. Later, however, finding the right colleague or peer to read it with, or at least discuss the ideas, can take thinking further. If it feels appropriate, someone else may see it with insight from a refreshingly different point of view, and perceive links, connections, developments, divergent perspectives or tangents.

Phase 1 writing probably will not be ready to be read critically in depth. Its lack of structure and grammatical form, because of the way it was created, makes it more appropriate for open discussion of its content and where the emerging ideas might lead. At its extreme Phase 1 might be completely unreadable by someone else (mine certainly is, and not only because it's in pencil). In such cases, a discussion about the ideas and concepts, or examples it has raised would be fruitful, rather than the other person or people reading the actual text.

These first discursive, supportive, confidential readers need to be chosen with care. We need to trust that they:

- Understand, and are happy to work with, the nascent nature of Phase 1 writing;
- Can be tentative and exploratory themselves;
- Can be relied upon to be confidential;
- Will treat my writing and ideas with respect, however wild and wacky and unformed they are at this stage.

This person, or small group, can become very significant within our writing lives. Communicating with my own first readers (different people for different genres) takes much time and care; I know the manuscripts I send out to publishers are qualitatively better in a range of ways than if they had not been through the careful hands of these much respected individuals. These relationships are reciprocal: I also read and comment on their manuscripts prior to publication.

Stephen

This is really important. I have often returned a proposed paper with the recommendation that the author ask a colleague to read it through. This applies at the early phases of writing as well as the final editing phase.

But many academics work in institutional environments with no such culture of collegial collaboration. I have worked in some departments where it is natural enough to ask a colleague down the corridor to read something and talk it through. But in others it can even be quite embarrassing to ask someone to help you out in this way. This is an important part of what is meant by a good research environment. It may be that there is little the individual can do about this. But it may be that one can take the initiative and set up a collaborative relationship with a colleague (or a small group) for the mutual support of writing.

Start a Reflective Research Journal

A *reflective research journal* is really no more than a holdall in which to throw and store ideas, concepts, quotes, musings and reflections. Some of the thoughts which course through us while we, say, conduct interviews or other data-gathering exercises, can be inspired. Yet if we don't grab them and write them down they are often lost. We all know what it's like to wake in the night trying to recapture that significant thought, and only manage to grasp the feeling of the idea. Well, if the research journal had been on hand at the time, or very soon after, it would have been recorded to be developed later.

The capacious holdall bag of the *research journal* can be ransacked for its gems at any time. It is not necessarily comprehensible to other readers as it is probably written in a Phase 1 type way. The ideas and concepts expressed and explored within it can however, as discussed above, be shared with the right carefully chosen reader(s).

Having gained strategies which open writing up and set it flowing, we turn in the next chapter to ones which help when we feel hopelessly blocked.

Don't just read: WRITE!

Here are activities that will help you move from thinking about writing to actually doing it.

1 Write (preferably on paper) in a free-flow way with no specific subject for *six minutes*, dumping whatever is in your mind onto the page. Do it every morning for at least a week. This is also a very effective way to begin every writing session (see above for full explanation and examples).

2 After each *six minute dump* writing session follow with at least ten minutes of focused writing. This might be about a theme you have planned beforehand, or it might be something which has arisen during the *six minutes* (see above for a full explanation).

3 Start a *Research Journal*. You might do this writing by hand in a notebook, or in a separate computer file. Use the *six minute* writing method, allowing yourself to reflect onto the page about any aspect of your research. Don't worry if it seems to diverge from being strictly about your research: you will perceive the relevance later.

4 Write about a time when you had an inspiration or moment of insight in your research, an experience relative to this publication. It could even be from ages ago. Allow yourself to write about the first occasion which comes to mind, or rather to hand; tell it as a narrative or story, putting in as much description and detail as seems to arise as you write: you will see the relevance of all this when you reread it later.

5 Write about your research in a:

- poem
- fairy story
- detective story
- whodunit
- comedy or pantomime
- small children's story
- mindmap (see www.mindmapping.com)
- collage of pictures cut from magazines
- drawing
- if your research were an animal, or a piece of furniture, or a food: what would it be? Write a descriptive paragraph or more (see above for more advice on this strategy).
- collect quotes that strike you from any source for a few days; can you incorporate them into your research; do they throw any light?

6 If you were stranded on a desert island, what would your essentials for writing be? Time would no longer be a problem. Allow yourself to dream. Write it as a story if you like.

And READ some more:

Bartholomae, D. (1985) 'Inventing the university', in M. Rose (ed.), *When a Writer Can't Write: Studies in Writer's Block and Other Composing Process Problems*. New York: Guilford. pp. 273–85.

Elbow, P. (1987) 'Closing my eyes as I speak: An argument for ignoring audience', *College English*, 49 (1): 50–69.

Academic writing is a special way of writing that pays particular attention to precision, the avoidance of ambiguity and disciplinary knowledge. This way of writing needs to be mastered in order to communicate research effectively. On the other hand, it may be that this very concern for a 'special' way of writing needs to be set aside so that we can gain a more straightforward sense of our meaning. Bartholomae emphasises the former view and Elbow the latter. Phase 1 writing is closer to Elbow's perspective, while the later editing phase acknowledges Bartholomae's view of academic 'discourse'.

Peseta, T. (2007) 'Troubling our desires for research and writing within the academic development project', *International Journal for Academic Development*, 12 (1): 15–23.

Research writing is increasingly valued in terms of its usefulness. This paper argues against this dominant assumption to consider other purposes.

5

Writer's Block

Writer's Block is an inadequate name for such a complex process. The word *block* gives the impression that it is an object in the path we can circumvent, blow up or climb over. It is a dynamic process, however, not a thing to be tackled head on. Such a subtle, slippery, ever-shifting process requires subtle sophisticated approaches. Writer's block is caused by lack of:

- time and energy management
- understanding how to manage periods of writing chaos
- three attitudes essential to good writing:
  - trust in the process of the three developmental phases of writing
  - confidence I can do it
  - self-respect to give myself appropriate conditions for this demanding work.

Seamus: Sometimes I don't feel like teaching. But I have to, and once I've started, it's usually fine. But with writing I somehow can only do it when I feel like it. Perhaps I just need the confidence to bash on regardless. But how? At times it just seems impossible. I know I should get on and do a *six minute write*, but I can't even make myself do that.

Helena: My life is complex, with many work and family commitments. It's really hard to settle down to really focused writing. And I know what I produce is patchy and bitty and – well not good – because of this. I could do with advice on time and energy management. And I so need help with boosting my confidence and dealing with those frightening times when it all seems a hopeless muddle.

> **Lee:** I love scientific research. Time disappears. Writing is different. Are the three phases also strategies for when I can't write? I want to feel more OK with my writing, and more secure that I am doing the right thing.
>
> **Joseph:** All the best writers get writer's block sometimes, so I guess I just have to wait until it goes. Trouble is, I waste quite a lot of time like that. I hope this chapter shows me how to manage things so I can be more disciplined when I get stuck.

How the Three Writing Phases Counteract Block

I have learned to write my way into writing, and out of writing blocks.

(Academic writing course member)

Trusting the phases can avoid some elements of writer's block in two main ways: developing a working writer's practice of working through the phases appropriately (this varies for every writer); feeling able to return to Phase 1 type writing at any time.

Write new material, redraft and edit at the right times

Each phase involves its own characteristic mode of thinking. Phase 1 writing is entirely for me, not for anyone else to read. So redrafting or editing (Phases 2, 3) when I should be writing first draft while it is flowing might prevent ideas and inspirations from tumbling out onto the page. Enormous quantities of energy, time and inspiration are wasted by writers beginning a writing session by neurotically working on earlier drafts, instead of simply rereading and moving forwards. This ongoing redrafting is a brake on developing new writing. Even worse is to try to edit at this early stage. Editing, which is trying to perfect style, grammar and punctuation, sorting out references accurately, and so on, will certainly block off creative inspiration. The worst example comes from fiction: Mr Casaubon in George Eliot's *Middlemarch* (1871) has a life project to write a tome and yet never gets beyond perfecting the first sentences.

Professional writers know this, and divide their time accordingly. Novelists, for example, will engage in creative Phase 1 writing when they know they have the appropriate energy (first thing in the morning for some, late at night for others), then go for a walk, and then later redraft, edit or write letters (in the afternoon if they've written all morning).

Writing new material (Phase 1) is demanding. Muddling the phases, and using prime-time energy for going back over work to improve it (Phases 2 or 3) at the wrong stage, is an avoidance tactic. Understanding the role of the phases enables us to let go of the need to polish and work up what we've already written, secure in the knowledge that it will be done: at the right time.

Return to Phase 1 type writing when necessary

Reflecting, by using Phase 1 type writing, is for exploring ideas and thoughts and inspiration. It can be fruitfully returned to at any time to sort through any problems, including 'I am stuck!' Reflecting on stuckness, seeking the ideas which seem to have vanished, can bring them to the fore again. This approach can work by using Phase 1 type writing which is genuinely explorative, reflective and not for anyone else to read. Here is one writer's experience:

> Struggle. What is this all about? Post shingles I have a complete lack of energy. I need to find my vital spirit again and the loss experienced by not being able to express myself through writing. So I thud anything onto the page in order to let go of this place I am in. I bring my tiredness to the page, my sorrow and open my heart to the possibility of renewal and discovery. I will write rubbish in order to delve beneath, to reach the depths of my being. I am stuck here unable to move, to progress so I throw these words on the page to get the pain out and rise above this place.
>
> (Lizzie)

If six minute type writing is not sufficiently unblocking, it can help to write a letter to the Writer Self. This aspect of ourselves is the one who writes lucidly, clearly and creatively. Such sought-after writing flow comes and goes seemingly according to its own laws for many writers. To gain more control over this side of myself, I find it valuable to write a letter to my Writer Self, asking her/him/it to sort it out. And then write the reply, allowing my hand to write as freely as I can. Those enduring a period of frustrating block find it useful to write to themselves from their Writer Self before beginning each writing session. Note how Bríd here uses the tin-opener questions introduced in Chapter 3.

> Dear Bríd
>
> Well, out with it, what are you trying to say? I know that you are trying to gather a few ideas in order to build an argument for the liberation agenda of

adult education. Your ultimate focus is on the practice of critical pedagogy. However, you want to link this to a wider social context, especially the inequality and injustice that creates educational disadvantage in the first place. ...

Now, narrow it down ...

Now, we should go for the Tin Opener questions: what is this paper about, why, when, how, where and who.

What: critical pedagogy, the approach to teaching and learning which recognises the unequal social structures in which all education takes place

Why: adult and community education has developed this approach, in particular, and I want to defend the role and provide a rationale for a wider practice.

When: this approach has developed over the past thirty years in particular, and the social conditions have been changing over this length of time too.

How: this will be a really useful section, as it will provide the position for an exploration of the practice.

Where: Ireland, looking back over a period of thirty years or so.

Who: radical educators, adult learners, HE and the field of adult and community education.

Now, where do we go from here? Well maybe the outline ...

Well, Bríd, what do you think? Have you something to go on? Will you be able to take up some of these strands? Write soon again!!

Bríd

(Bríd Connolly)

Building confidence

Confidence is almost as slippery as writer's block itself. I might think I'm confident in my research, in my findings and theories, but when it comes to putting them down, either what comes out seems thin, or doesn't express what I wanted to communicate, or is rejected by peer reviewers for reasons I don't know how to respond to. What's going on?

Or I might be aware of crippling lack of confidence. I just can't write and know that whatever I put on the page will be rubbish, and so it proves. When I first did big keynote lectures and was very nervous, someone said to me: 'Your audience are all on your side. They really want to hear what you have to say, otherwise they wouldn't have come.' I learned readers are also on my side. And it's true.

Through all this I'm working out who is in charge. Am I the writer in charge of my writing? Or is my writing in charge of me? If I am in charge, I can write with confidence and authority.

Our minds are rich storehouses. Effective writing relies on our being able to move in and out of this storehouse, taking what we need when we need it. When this process is working smoothly, we do not notice it, but we do notice the effect.

> I get a nice adrenaline rush when the writing goes smoothly, and a sense of satisfaction when I'm reasonably happy with it.
>
> (Academic writing course member)

This storehouse is huge, much larger than we are ever aware. Let me give you an analogy. The Royal Opera House in Covent Garden London, from which I am lucky enough to live a few minutes' walk (and therefore know how to get cheap tickets), has a beautiful stage and atmospheric crimson and gold auditorium. I am allowed into the auditorium; I would soon be stopped if I tried to go on the stage or beyond. Yet beyond the velvet curtains is about 9 acres of working space: rehearsal halls, green rooms, offices, canteens, storage spaces, costume design, creation, repair studios, etc. This private area is far greater than the front of house. Without this massive space, there would be no well-loved world-class opera or ballet visible from the auditorium.

Our minds are rather like this. We live our everyday lives in a public space where we relate to others in ways we've been socialised. When we start to write or reflect internally on writing we need to create routes of access to the huge areas of our minds which hold what we have learned, discovered, thought through, invented, wondered about. This area is generally closed, to facilitate the most effective normal everyday functioning. Stephen often thinks deeply about his writing, rather than writing it down in Phase 1 type writing. He was thus engaged once, following a lecture. Unfortunately he was also crossing a busy London street, and stepped straight into the path of a car, and so severely fractured his ankle it had to be pinned in several places, causing lasting impairment of movement. I suspect the poor shocked car driver assumed he was either mad in the ordinary way, or a mad professor.

So, how to ensure we can gain access to this storehouse appropriately? The late British Poet Laureate Ted Hughes reckoned he had to 'outwit his own inner police system, which told him what is permissible, what is possible, what is "him"' (1982: 7). His 'inner police' tried to instruct him how he should be; tried to keep him within the safe space of the auditorium of his mind (because critical creativity takes us dangerously close to boundaries, sometimes even over barriers, sometimes even exposing us to severe injury). Ted Hughes suggested writers use 'games' to enable this outwitting. The *six minute dump* is one of the best and simplest strategies for such outwitting, as Lizzie pointed out above. The many exercises in *Inspirational Writing* develop this: writing to and from the Writer Self (see above) is one, and there are more at each chapter end.

The novelist and critic Virginia Woolf fought a domestic angel inside her head, who tried to mould her into the Victorian ideal mother and wife (sister and aunt, etc.) living her life selflessly in the service always of others. Writing was anathema to this angel, because it is a 'selfish' activity.

> The Angel in the House ... excelled in the difficult arts of family life. She sacrificed herself daily ... so constituted that she never had a mind or wish of her own, but preferred to sympathise always with the minds and wishes of others ... The shadow of her wings fell on my page ... directly I took my pen in my hand ... she slipped behind me and ... made as if to guide my pen ... I turned upon her and caught her by the throat. I did my best to kill her. She would have plucked the heart out of my writing ... It is far harder to kill a phantom than a reality. She was always creeping back when I thought I had despatched her.

> (Woolf, 1979 [1931]: 60)

Hughes and Woolf were brilliant writers, but neither biddable nor socially conformist: they tackled their destructive inner police for the sake of their work. They can be models for us: in the pursuit of critical exploration we can locate our own inner police, and destroy or develop strategies to outwit them. Giving this blocking power metaphorical form (police, cloying domestic angel) can help put flesh on its bones.

An academic writer, less likely to be haunted by *the angel in the house*, is perhaps policed by needing to tackle the daily business of teaching, lecturing, responding to departmental directives. Writing only too often takes second place with substandard energy, and so gets put off and put off ...

So-called mind-readers tune their senses to pick up as much as possible of the information other people give unintentionally about their thoughts and feelings. They use these clues to make it seem they know what people are thinking. We writers make mind-readers of ourselves. Phase 1 writing can help us become more aware of what's going on around us and in our own heads: what we know and understand without realising it. We habitually live our lives only noticing a narrow range of information. The storehouses in our minds remain locked and bolted, the Opera House nine acres remains inaccessibly behind that thick curtain, and my writing suffers.

'It is far harder to kill a phantom than a reality.' Yes, but there are strategies for communicating with this phantom: far more powerful than trying to silence and destroy a formless nagging in the mind.

Periods of Writing Chaos

Good writing is the result of 99% perspiration and 1% inspiration.

(Thomas Edison)

All writing, particularly academic, has times when it seems a complete muddle with no possible order, ever. There is so much wildly disparate and dislocated stuff, and yet it all has to have a proper place in the publication. This is the opposite sort of confidence loss to the stuck 'I've got nothing to write, nothing of importance or interest to say'. That block is negative: there's nothing there. This block is all too positive: there's far too much, and I have no idea how to sort it out and never will.

How do I get through this loss of confidence? After all the years I've been writing, I know I have to stay with this intensely uncomfortable stage, even though every voice I can hear in my head is saying: 'you can't do it Gillie, give up and do housework/embroidery/write something easier and non-academic'. I get through it by knowing the above adage about perspiration and inspiration is true: I have to stick my bottom to the chair and doggedly carry on sorting, finding connections, seeking the bit which seems to work the best and starting there rather than with the totally intractable part. This latter will suddenly slide into place once I've got the difficult but not totally impossible bits more sorted. I often look back on a publication with amazement, remembering this terrible chaotic stage: no one would ever guess the total despair I had felt. In fact, editing this now, this is exactly what I feel about *Inspirational Writing*.

Time and Energy Management

The intensity of academic writing requires much energy, time and commitment, and therefore effective strategies for their management.

My life with its many parts (being an academic writer, poet, journal keeper, grandmother, mother, wife, lecturer, sister, ...) can be likened to a mansion with many rooms, attics, corridors, gardens and terraces. Many doors get left open: this is OK as long as I know which room or garden I need to be in, and where essential equipment has been left or stored. These open doors too often are to rooms or spaces demanding my attention, however. Children are shrieking in one, something burns in the kitchen, the vine has blown off the wall and needs pinning back, a dandelion is swamping a delicate plant and needs weeding out, the fire has thrown sparks on the rug. So we rush from room to room, down corridors, inside and outside, from flower bed to vegetable garden, never really moving forward, just round and round dealing with crises. Yet, with care and forethought, I can close doors, trusting everything's OK behind them. I can go confidently through one door, and shut it behind me to focus properly, with the right materials to hand.

The metaphor is clear; now how do I turn this image into real-life actions? How do I prevent myself from feeling I must keep up with my emails all the time; my computer flashes each one at me in the corner, my former computer beeped. Can I really turn off my mobile (cell) phone? Can I really leave until tomorrow preparing for that imminent lecture/meeting? The deadline for this publication is a long way off, whereas everything else is needed now, or even yesterday.

This pressure from other things demanding to be done first, to be done with the best energy of the morning, is hard to resist, because they are far easier to do. I am half way through my emails before I realise I sat down to tackle that tricky chapter. Many have told me that when they work on a difficult part at home rather than in the office, their house is clean and tidy, or the dripping tap fixed. If I'm writing something hard I find I have to make nourishing soup or a complex salad for my lunch; if the writing's whizzing, I don't eat.

Author Jonathan Franzen is reported to have sealed up the internet connection to his computer; Zadie Smith has said she uses two software programs to block access to distracting specific websites. Dan Brown undertakes inversion therapy by hanging upside down wearing gravity boots to help him relax and concentrate (Henley, 2013: 3). Stephen King writes to loud hard-rock music, but has no telephone, TV or videogames in his writing room where every distraction like a view from the window is eliminated (King, 2000).

Stephen King (2000), like Virginia Woolf (1942), says he, and most writers he knows, write best in their own place, however basic or humble. He says the most important element of his private space is being willing to shut the door, and to make sure everyone knows it's firmly shut.

Heather has been struggling to manage all the demanding elements in her life: writing not only a book based on her PhD, but also personal journal, fiction, lectures and papers, etc. Here is her dialogue with her writer-self: *she* is her non-academic-writer-self who wants to get on with writing fiction; Heather the academic is 'I'.

What can I do? I whisper almost desperately. I am far too spineless, following good intentions is not easily put into practice. And yet I sense the seriousness of this situation.

'We need to negotiate', she says 'rather than fight for the same hours, moments, energy sources. Heather the Academic is able to bring in the discipline. Heather the Writer has the voice and the narrative skill. So, let's make a clear plan.'

I'm amazed and yet fully with her. She is in my mind and I am in hers. Yet, the clarity of these roles and their destructive sides has never been on paper as it is now.

The Academic needs the Writer, especially in the mornings. So, we'll start with her writing, personal pages and fiction writing. I'm to give her an hour in the morning through more efficient morning routines. Then I'll smoothly move onto my research paper. One at a time, so that I feel the sense of accomplishment. I know that too well. I developed a habit of planning overly many research papers, never clearly finishing them off. Postponing, writing, forgetting, warming up. Vicious cycle where nothing is ready, nothing is new, nothing is inviting to work with. Yes, I can change that. Only at lunch hour, she says I'm to work with my emails, NOT BEFORE.

So, what is my experiment? I will be writing for the first hour with her. Her stories as she likes them. Giving them space to arise. Then I will work on my research papers or book until lunchtime and digesting my emails only after that. News are for the later afternoon. I am not the school girl who once tried to get things right, avoid mistakes or even was afraid of mistakes. Now all that is gone.

I'm breathing more freely, lighter and yet more in me. This is my year to write and I can do it!

(Heather)

Another fruitful strategy is to think through what kind of writer I am, so I can work out what works best for me. Here are some suggestions:

- Give myself the luxury of materials I like, and which suit me, the right lamp …
- Sit properly and comfortably. Allow myself breaks, exercise, light relief.
- Choose the right place for different types of writing: office, kitchen, library, bed.
- Discover my pattern, the right times and pace for me: 6 am or midnight; quick bursts …
- Pile stuff out of sight, list and file my mind's clutter to deal with later.
- Use my best energy for writing. Schedule writing sessions into prime time.
- Be kind and generous to myself, especially in the first phases. Later I need to be thoroughly critical, but not yet.

- Give myself constant small rewards AFTER some writing has been achieved. Get up and look out of the window for a few minutes, fetch an apple to munch, walk around the garden or block.
- Every writer has delaying strategies. Mine is emails. For one successful novelist it's all her household chores.
- Distinguish between delaying tactics and times of allowing my mind off the leash to sprout and mature ideas, such as going for a walk.
- I can tell colleagues/children/staff I am unavailable for half-an-hour/six months.
- I can ignore emails. My telephone can be switched off too (even mobile/cell phone).
- Leave my work each session at an interesting beginning of something. I push myself to begin to work on the next section before I stop for the day, or at least list significant points to work on tomorrow. I bless myself for giving myself something to start from next time.
- What's all-time best? Being open to surprise. Being willing to enter uncharted waters. Writing without prior thinking. Being Bold.

Stephen

I have a love–hate relationship with writing: it's an obsessive-compulsive disorder. When I am involved in writing anything from a personal letter to a book, I cannot get it out of my head. I'll wake up in the middle of the night thinking about how the next bit might go, or something that needs changing. If it's a long project, the writing will become the central part of my life.

But once it's finished, the feeling of relief is liberating. I have had four academic books published, and I can remember that after each one I said I never wanted to write another book.

I have found that these movements between loving writing and hating it became a cyclical process in my academic work. At times when I love writing I am much more focused on what Gillie has described as Phases 2 and 3: I feel in contact with my audience and try to articulate my ideas with precision so that they can become a contribution to the wider world of ideas. In the periods when I hate writing, my creativity is much more unbounded: new crazy ideas emerge, new angles on a research problem, even new directions. At these times my ideas are much too fluid to control for communicating in writing. I'll talk to people a lot about things, read from quite different disciplinary areas and explore new research methods. This period corresponds much more closely to Gillie's Phase 1, in which I am struggling for clarity for myself.

This dynamic relationship between my writing and my ideas only became clear to me later in my career. I began to notice that there were periods of two or three years when I would publish a lot, and other periods when I published nothing. Unfortunately, the former did not necessarily coincide with institutional and research assessment. It took time and confidence to learn to trust my own cyclical creative process and not be bullied by institutional demands. In the end that paid off, I like to think.

The consequences of this cyclical process upon the practical details of how I write are unusual. When I was in a writing period I would invariably write in my office with my door open. Since I knew that I was totally 'held' by my writing, the interruptions of other people coming in to my room were not a distraction but a pleasant interlude. I would happily engage for a while in a discussion of institutional politics, or some detail about a curriculum issue, knowing that as soon as the conversation ended I would return to my writing refreshed at the exact point I left it. At other times I would attempt to engage the interrupting colleague with the very issue I was writing about and there were several times when the ideas from these coincidental encounters emerged in my final text.

I rarely wrote at home. Although I often woke at night thinking about a problem, I never continued the writing at home. I now think that the reason for this separation is that if I were to allow writing to take place at home then it would completely dominate my life for those writing periods. Another advantage of my unusual approach is that I have always related very positively to my office as a space in which my ideas have developed. Making my office 'mine' in this way has, to some extent, insulated me from the worst institutional pressures which otherwise are anti-intellectual.

My writing is therefore not readily controlled by me, nor by my institutional context. Research assessment exercises, for example, have had little impact one way or another upon it. Creativity – albeit obsessive and neurotic at times – cannot be altogether manageable.

Having made a start tackling writers' most besetting problems, the next section turns to writing's Phase 2. Phase 1 concerned achieving and maintaining a flow of first-draft writing by focusing on what I know, and think I want to say. We next find out what our readers want to hear.

 Don't just read: WRITE!

Here are activities that will help you move from thinking about writing, to actually doing it.

1 Write (preferably on paper) in a free-flow way with no specific subject for *six minutes*, dumping whatever is in your mind onto the page. Do it every morning for at least a week. This is also a very effective way to begin every writing session (see above for full explanation and examples).
2 When your writing's stuck, go somewhere other than your desk, anywhere which strikes your fancy. Follow on from this beginning in a *six minute dump* way:
   What I am really trying to say here is …
3 Complete these sentence stems, writing as much or as little as seems appropriate:

   - I really do not feel like writing now because …
   - I am bored with my writing because …

- No one will ever publish it because …
- I would MUCH rather be …

4 Think of an occasion you found yourself doing anything other than write during a set-aside writing time. What were you doing and why? What was stopping you write? Use the *six minute dump* method to reflect upon who your equivalent of the police system or angel-in-the-house were (see above for more information and examples).

5 Write a letter to your Writer Self, asking her/him/it to sort out your current writing problem. Write the reply, allowing your hand to write freely as far as you can (see above for more information).

6 Write a list of strategies which might help you get down to writing productively on any occasion without procrastinating or being distracted (see above for more information and examples).

And READ some more:

Boice, R. (1990) *Professors as Writers: A Self-Help Guide to Productive Writing.* Oklahoma: New Forums Press Inc.
This self-help manual for academics who want to write more productively, painlessly and successfully reflects the author's two decades of experience and research with academics as writers. Like the actual sessions and workshops in which the author works with writers, this book admonishes and reassures as a kind of 'therapy session' on writing blocks.

Evans, K. (2013) *Pathways through Writing Blocks in the Academic Environment.* Rotterdam: Sense Publishers.
This is a playful creative approach to unblocking writing, with plenty of strategies and exercises to try.

Phase 2: Focused Redrafting

6

Redraft for my Reader

We now turn from communicating solely with ourselves, to communicating as effectively and interestingly as possible with our readers. Phase 2 writing addresses how writers' relationships with readers are vital for the publication to be appropriately focused. We start with working out who the reader of each specific publication is, what they want from it and how to engage critically with them. We then consider their initial engagement with the publication: the title.

Seamus: I can always visualise a seminar group of students to help me plan a session. But how do I visualise my readers and have a sense of their interests and needs? And how do I know if they've grasped what I'm getting at?

Helena: I feel so much lighter about writing now. But my supervisor says she feels it doesn't communicate to her at all clearly. I've got to get out of my own head and see how someone else might read my writing. But I don't know my PhD examiner! How do I know what will interest her/him? And how do I know how to make it clear to them?

Lee: OK, I feel more confident. But how can this get my publications cited and quoted? What exactly do readers want to learn from my research, so they then cite and quote me? Can I find that out? Can I write it so they understand? And I need to write a clear title.

Joseph: How do I get my ideas across to the great intellectuals in my field? OK, well if the Big Names don't actually get round to reading my stuff, then who will? And how can I make sure they're the right sort of people?

Who is my Reader?

Every reader asks of every publication 'So what?', 'What difference will this make to me and my thinking and research, and my place in the field?'

> Once I realised that I was writing to communicate something to an external audience, my work began to be accepted for publication. ... Scholarship is conversation.
>
> (Huff, 1999: ix, 3)
>
> I wanted to open up my research writing to make it accessible to the general public (non-specialist readership).
>
> I'm so glad I wrote ALL my thoughts and ideas and inspirations and hesitations at phase one. It's surprising now I'm thinking about who is going to read this and just what they want to know, I'm certain I'd have missed out a lot of what I now know they will want to read.
>
> (Academic writing course members)

We now work out who our readers are, and focus the publication towards them. Readers might be unknown academics, editors, peer reviewers, examiners or supervisors. A first draft has been written, expressing much of what I want to say, and perhaps a bit more. Now a great writer's skill comes into play: working out how to address the particular readers of this specific publication. Because each publication has a readership with its own wants and needs. This focus enables me to write clear prose which succeeds in communicating my data, theory and views. My publication will contribute significantly to the field of knowledge if I can engage my readers as people within that field.

Who are you, my reader?

Why do you want to read this?

Why do I want to say this to you?

How do I think you are going to read it?

What are you most interested in, out of what I want to say?

Where and when can I publish, so that my publication speaks to you?

Gaining knowledge of who our readers are means focusing the publication towards them, engaging them with appropriate language and form. This can have the effect of making the writing come to life for these readers.

It's rare however for a writer to know who precisely their readers will be; even a doctoral thesis is for an unknown examiner until very near the viva. We therefore have to imagine readers as clearly as we can. The following exercise, which I do at every academic writers' course, can really help to bring them to life.

Reader Visualisation Exercise

- Think of someone you've met at a conference or other appropriate occasion, depending what you're writing.
- In your mind's eye, sit them in front of you to hear what you have to say.
- Take the largest piece of paper available (preferably A1, though, if this feels daunting, A4 will do).
- Draw your reader(s) boldly, perhaps with felt-tip pens. Stick figures can be pretty expressive if, like me, drawing isn't your strong point.

One group of primary care nurses noticed a common characteristic in their reader-portraits: they all had big sensible shoes. Clearly all their imagined readers were practical practitioners.

Stephen

PhD students appear to have three rather different audiences: supervisor(s), examiners and academic community. Examiners are rather like journal peer referees or reviewers, but the supervisor is rather different. Sometimes a student will write for me (rather than for the other readers) and that is fine so long as it helps them think through ideas. But often I will play the role of an examiner, who would not have the same intimate knowledge of the research process or the researcher and thus whose engagement would need to be elicited.

What does my Reader Want to Know?

Next we seek to know what will absorb our readers, and what their voice is like. The next two exercises develop not only appropriate content, but also a clear lucid writing style.

Letters to and from readers, Exercise 1

- Write a letter to your reader, asking them what they want from your writing.
- Then write the reply, making this response as long and full as you can because this letter might well form the basis of the introduction to your writing.

Stephen

I was stuck with writing at the very beginning of a book, for which I had a contract. I just couldn't think of how to start. Gillie suggested I write a letter to the reader. I thought this was a silly idea, but she pushed me. Once I had started it was difficult to stop. When I did, Gillie suggested I write my reader's response to my letter. I did. The first chapter was soon written. It was not that I now knew something I didn't know before, or that I now realised what subject matter was relevant for the start, but just that I had a feeling of engagement with my reader. As if I had made them into a human being that I wanted to talk to, rather than just a figment of my imagination.

Listen to two other writers' response to the letters:

I found the profound effectiveness of the letter and response exercise gave me a different way to connect with the material I'm working with. I found when I came to write the first reply from my reader that I hadn't formulated who he/she was clearly enough; so a large part of my reply writing was working out who it was from. That jolted me out of my little 'speaking only to myself' box!

Then the letters from my reader were deeply critical and questioning. She/he asked questions I hadn't thought of, and questioned the assumptions which underpin my current writing. At first my reader was too critical and harsh, like my internal terrorist. So I engaged my internal mentor to soften this voice, and then I very quickly found out what I'd left out: my reader said I had to find the burning heart of my writing. That was my weak point! In fact it was that I was not asking 'why?' enough: I was not being sufficiently critical.

(Sunita)

I had almost given up in despair with writing up my thesis. It was 320,000 words long in draft, and I could not see how I had got myself so tangled up in the text. The 'write a letter' exercise was one of the most useful self-help tools I could have been provided with, and over the next six months became a constant tool whenever I felt stuck or frozen in my rewriting. Here is part of my letter to my critical first reader about my problem of having very different final readers of my PhD thesis.

Hi Alison,

I've been working on my PhD literature review, trying to link together the theories we've been talking about over the past few months. As always I seem to be stuck, not because I don't understand the theories, but because I know I have two audiences, and I am so painfully aware of these. ...

The H.E. marker will be familiar with constructivism and, with any luck the mixed qualitative studies that distinguish phenomenography from phenomenology. ... Can I talk about constructivist findings at the same time as phenomenographic ones without explaining the differences? And what on earth will a philosopher/pragmatic linguistic specialist make of all the edubabble?

(Bernadette Knewstubb)

Letters to and from readers, Exercise 2

- Write a letter to a reader with no knowledge at all about the issues or subject of the publication.
- Be absolutely clear about every element of the subject: there can be no fudging and no missing out of any links, because this reader will rapidly become confused.

Arlene and 'Anon' gained a great deal of clarity from this exercise:

The process of writing to a novice helped me clarify what I am really trying to say. Here it is:

We have been investigating methods to deliver a biological control agent to the brushtail possum in New Zealand. The number of brushtail possums in New Zealand has become too high and they are now a pest animal. We need more humane ways to control them than using poisons. A biological control agent is something that will reduce the number of possums by decreasing their breeding (or killing them). A very important aspect of this work is to test the delivery system in the live possum. We have produced hollow particles with polymer walls that are in the nanometer size range (a nanometer is very small, a fraction of a millimetre). We can load the biological control agent inside these particles and then we have put these particles in the gut of possums. We can then see if we can measure any of the entrapped biological control agent in the blood of possums. Once in the bloodstream, the biocontrol agent is able to perform the biological role of causing the animal to be sterile, for example. Eventually we hope to be able to make a bait containing the nanoparticles that the animal will eat.

(Arlene McDowell)

My letter to a First Year Undergraduate was a way of gaining clarity:

Randomised Controlled Trials need to have and keep a large sample (the people taking part in the trial) so that findings are statistically valid. Getting the sample is called recruitment; keeping it is called retention. To successfully recruit a sample you need to know: how many you want to recruit; who (what sort of people) you want to recruit; how you plan to recruit them. There are a number of models to do this. A social marketing model is discussed here.

71

Now we need to keep them involved. If there is too much attrition or 'drop out' the validity of the results will be called into question. Retaining participants requires a deep understanding of the reasons people stay involved, especially if the trial does not necessarily have a positive, or any, effect on them. So, while people may initially seek to get something out of participation for themselves, their family or community, loyalty needs to be built to the research itself. This requires an environment where participants view their role as important and their continued participation as having a direct and critical impact on the whole research process.

So retention works on philosophical and practical levels. The philosophical relates to the level of ownership of and commitment to the project, the practical to what barriers to participation need to be removed and supports put in place.

(Anon)

These two letter-writing exercises help us speak authentically in writing to a specific readership. With the insights gained from them, we are unlikely to write like this:

Many people, faced with putting their thoughts on paper, adopt a new, and usually unattractive, personality. Most of us can communicate effectively over the dinner table or in our local pub, but once we start writing we are all tempted to use a completely different set of words and constructions. This may come from a conscious desire to impress, or a subconscious regression to schooldays, when teachers gave higher praise for longer words. Whatever the cause, the results are awful.

(Albert, 1992: 45)

Does my Reader Hear What I Want them to Hear?

Being aware of my reader in relationship to me can greatly help the clarity and appropriateness of the content of what I write. I still cannot determine precisely what a reader will hear, however. Readers bring experience and feelings to their relationship with a publication, which are inevitably different from the writer's.

A publication does not always communicate what its writer wished, sometimes more, sometimes less, sometimes even something entirely different from what they intended. A text is very much more than a medium for the transmission of information. Writing and reading are both creative interpretive acts involving cognitive, emotional and sometimes spiritual faculties of both writer and reader. The writer and reader are likely to draw on different emotional and cognitive forces. Writers cannot determine what readers will understand from their writing; they can try their hardest, however, to say what they mean and mean what they say as clearly and fully as possible. This reminds me of the child, with a child's understanding of the world, who called his teddy Gladly. When asked why, he replied 'his eyes aren't quite right, like in the hymn in church' ('Gladly the cross I'd bear').

Keeping focus

What the reader wants to hear from me, is as significant as *how* to address them. Each publication has its own range of readers, with their own wants and needs. One thing is always constant, however, whatever the specific interests and material:

- Readers are interested in what I have to tell them about my research.
- Readers are not interested in me as a person.

Phase 1 writing is the time to work through personal involvements in the subject of writing. This might be emotional; Stephen said: 'But while anger may often fuel writing, I think it is vital that anger is not expressed in academic writing (at least, not normally). To do so would be to confuse the fuel with the fire.' The expression of other raw and unresolved emotions is equally inappropriate.

Stephen

Some kinds of research reports do involve discussion of the researcher's feelings where relevant to the research methods. For example, a social scientist interviewing a subject may come to realise they were influenced by hostile feelings. Such self-critical reflexive comment may be important to take account of and report. But reporting on anger is quite different from being angry on the page.

My personal involvement with my subject might not find its way into the writing as expressed emotion, but perhaps as a side alley of anecdote which fascinates me – yet, upon examination at Phase 2, I realise it is of little interest to my reader. Publications for non-disciplinary readerships do very appropriately contain anecdotes which can lucidly illustrate an otherwise incomprehensibly abstruse subject, if they are chosen with care. Or the inappropriate material might be personal information (this is academic writing not memoir).

'I believe …' is also inappropriate personal involvement because academic readers want to know the critical foundation of arguments and theories, not the personal beliefs of the writer. Readers are interested in what we have to tell them, not in us personally in any way at all. It is the text, rather than the author, which 'lives' (Barthes, 1977; Foucault, 1984).

Focus, focus, focus

Research and scholarly study is generally more widely focused than a particular publication arising from it. Selecting the appropriate line of argument, and specific data from the wealth the study has thrown up, is not always straightforward. I tend to get overenthusiastic and want to tell my readers everything in the first publication, for example. But however brilliant it all seems, I have to keep focus on what readers want from this particular publication, and reserve all the rest of the material for a future publication.

Involving readers critically

Academic readers' relationships with the publications they read are always critical, wanting to further their own knowledge, experience and understanding. They want full information about every finding, all data, the source of every statement. We owe it to these readers, as well as to our standing in the field, to substantiate every statement we make. Our readers are likely to use the tin openers (see pp. 34–5) about our publications, asking: Why is he saying this? What's her authority? How does he know this? When, where, from whom did she gain this information? Making unsubstantiated claims is a certain route to losing relationships with readers: if they suspect the writer of such unscholarly actions, they will put the publication down and not continue reading.

A way of drawing academic readers into dialogic relationship is to include some critique of the argument, dataset, or methods. Every researcher has hesitations about what they've done or not done, about the threads of argument they have not followed (because we can't follow them all). This kind of critique is an essential element in research: leaving it out in publications creates a gap which readers are aware of, even if not consciously. Including reference to these kinds of critiques involves readers critically in these trains of thought, which has the beneficial effect of strengthening both the argument, and the relationship with readers.

A Communication Loop

Ideally every publication creates a feedback loop:

Me the writer → my text → my reader → feedback → me.

Feedback can reach us in different ways. Direct contact is one, via email for example when a journal publishes the author's address, or readers gain contact with authors in other ways.

Discussing, quoting or citing in a further publication is another really satisfying form of feedback. This can be a genuine continuation of conversation: a reader writes, building upon what they've read; this writing is read by the original writer. The discussion frequently goes on from there: another reader picks up the clues from this first reader and responds in their own way. As the original writer I might then re-enter the conversation, which has by now been taken interestingly further than I'd envisaged.

Stephen

The idea of academic writing as being a contribution to a conversation is important, but it can be rather sobering to realise how often such conversation is merely a possibility rather than a reality. Research a while ago showed the average academic paper is read by 2.6 people. I'm not sure if that included or excluded the two referees. But either way, this doesn't sound much like a very lively conversation. I found it useful to forget this when writing a paper.

The Power of the Title

Titles are a vital element in the communication. I'd like to imagine my reader posing me a question in as short a form as they can. What does he or she want to know? I listen to the type of words and constructions my reader uses in her question. This helps me frame a working (draft) title. The best titles not only catch readers' imaginations, they also catch writers'. It can therefore be inspiring to acquire a strong working title early on. We can be respected researchers and inspirational writers at the same time: the title is the first place to display that both to prospective readers and to ourselves in our relationship with our writing.

Exercise for creating a working title

- Write a newspaper headline about the subject of a draft publication.
- Add a powerful verb.

Here is an academic writing course participant's headline:

Classroom interactions vital for critical thinking development

(Rob Wass)

Adding the strongest appropriate verb (action word) might turn this into a title. The simplest would be 'are' ('Classroom interactions *are* ...'). But that gives a very unpunchy title. 'Classroom interactions develop critical thinking' might do the job, and at the same time turn a noun into a verb – generally a dynamic thing to do. I'm sure Rob found something even stronger.

Verbs are the doing words, and therefore perhaps the most significant in a sentence: they really do have to be as strong as possible. Here is one writer's feelings:

Finding the right verb (through a brainstorming technique) completely shifted my perspective on what the subject of my topic was 'doing'. This strategy was not an attack, but rather a seduction, which is perhaps why it was so effective.

(Academic writing course member)

Finding possible readers not only focuses the writing, it also gives confidence. Once I can picture some typical readers I know they are keen to find out what I have to say. They are on my side; if they weren't they wouldn't read what I've written. This gives me much greater confidence in expressing myself in writing.

 Don't just read: WRITE!

Here are activities that will help you move from thinking about writing, to actually doing it.

1 Write (preferably on paper) in a free-flow way with no specific subject, for *six minutes*, dumping whatever is in your mind onto the page. Do it every morning for at least a week. This is also a very effective way to begin every writing session (see above for full explanation and examples).
2 Make a list of your potential readers, they might be real people, or categories. Choose your most 'typical' reader from your list.
   Draw a picture (stick figures perhaps) of him or her, preferably on a large sheet of paper with thick pens such as board markers.
   If possible discuss this drawing with a critical friend or colleague to try to understand better who your reader is (see above for more advice and an example).

3 Write a letter to your typical reader, asking them what they want from your publication, and what they see as the critiques of the research you describe and discuss in it. Write the reply (see above for more information and examples).

4 Now write to a reader who knows little or nothing about your subject area, an undergraduate student or lay person perhaps. Explain what you are writing about in ways they will understand (see above for more information and examples).

5 Create a list of questions for your reader. They can be anything.
   Now write the answers.
   Now write a list of questions posed by your reader, and answer them.

6 Write a newspaper headline for your draft publication.
   Now add a dynamic, yet appropriate verb. This is a draft for your title (see above for more advice, and examples).

And READ some more:

Barthes, R. (1975) *The Pleasure of the Text,* trans. R. Howard. New York: Hill & Wang.
Barthes makes a distinction between readerly texts, in which the reader is largely a passive recipient of a fixed text, and writerly texts which engage the reader in a continual process of interpretation and reinterpretation. Barthes argues for the importance of the latter. It raises the interesting question of the extent to which academic writing aims to be fixed in its meanings, or open to different meanings depending upon the position of the reader.

Rocco, T., Hatcher, T. et al. (eds) (2011) *The Handbook of Scholarly Writing and Publishing.* San Francisco, CA: John Wiley.
This useful book includes a good chapter on focusing on the audience for writing.

7

Engage Critically

Good academic writing engages critically with its subject by asking searching questions of it. *Engaging critically* involves tussling and searching and seeking to understand the endless questions within intellectual enquiry (particularly those beginning with 'why?'), an absorbing process. This chapter also addresses how to find the right environment and the right colleagues with whom to read and discuss our writing critically.

Seamus: People who are interested in teaching readily share their experience in a supportive way, I find. Researchers, on the other hand, are inclined to be more competitive. I'd like to share my writing more, but feel a bit anxious about it. How can I feel more a part of a supportive writing community?

Helena: What is the difference between explaining and describing something I'm interested in, and writing academically? I can see it's not just about clever words, which I had thought it was. And how do I fit in all this stuff I'm reading: it's fascinating, but I can't just do a list of 'Smith and Bloggs said …', can I? I feel so alone in all this, it feels a bit like a vast desert with no oases. Now breathe deeply, Helena: I do know how to engage critically with people about paintings! Surely it's much the same?

Lee: I just write up my research, don't I? What is this 'engaging critically?' Do I need to engage critically with readers? And if so, how? I am worried about doing this on my own now. My writing has been with a team before. They helped me get it right. How can I know if it is OK on my own?

> **Joseph:** In theory, I like the idea of other people reading and commenting on my work. The trouble is finding the right kind of people who share my perspective. There's no point sharing my ideas with some sort of positivist from the Dark Ages. I hope this chapter helps me to find the right kind of critical collaborators who will ask the right kind of questions.

Critical engagement is one of the most significant elements of academic writing, the one most worth working on. It is also the element many people struggle with communicating succinctly and clearly. As well as addressing questions which are thought to be significant, a critical engagement challenges commonly accepted assumptions. It often raises new questions which had not previously been thought to be significant. This is the second most significant element of academic writing: it must take nothing for granted and must challenge commonly and personally held assumptions.

A critical approach also asks significant questions of the surrounding field, the relationship between this field and the research being reported, and the implications to the field of this research with its new ideas and theories. This relationship with the field is often given the uninspiring name 'literature review', as if it were a mechanical process: it isn't; it is dynamic and critical.

Developing a critically engaging approach, and expressing it lucidly, is the biggest challenge academic writing has to offer.

If academic writing is a conversation with other academics, then gaining interlocutors can begin even before publication. There's nothing to beat developing a community of writers willing and able to read each other's drafts, and comment critically and positively upon them. Or at least one first critical reader to bounce ideas off and have intense discussions based on pieces of writing.

Asking the Critical Questions

The tin opener question stems (why, how, what, who, where, when) were introduced in Chapter 3. We will begin here with *Why*, because this stem introduces intellectual, philosophical questions. If *why* is iteratively asked again of every answer to each *why* question, then a truly philosophical train of enquiry will ensue. It is the process of the natural (or child) philosopher. Einstein reckoned he was able to elucidate relativity because he was a slow developer; as an adult he asked questions most people grow out of asking (those endless 'why's of the child).

As writers we succeed by engaging fully with what specifically we have the authority to say, to whom, how, where (which publication), when and – why: this last critical element is often missed out, leading to so many academic publications being really boring and un-enquiring.

Asking Why? asks for argument, leading to a critical engagement with the material presented. Academic writing is too often seen as 'writing up' the facts: reporting how, who, what, where, when (data, findings and so on). To gain attention, and to create a significant contribution to its field, an academic publication has to be a discussion, an argument. It has to engage in why this research was undertaken, also why it was necessary, and why readers should fully engage, and cite it.

Asking why relentlessly also pushes us to examine what we take for granted, and what assumptions underlie the field where our research belongs. These are among the most critically significant questions we can ask.

Claire Collins, a doctoral student, came to me puzzled and stuck. Her research was to investigate the usefulness of reflective practice to psychology counselling trainees. I asked her to respond to the simple question Why? She was planning to interview several trainees but hadn't thought of asking them directly 'Why do you reflect?', nor had she asked herself 'Why do I want to undertake this study? Why is it of interest to me?' Listen to what it felt like to her:

> I felt that something was missing in my research interviews, that I still hadn't nailed the point so to speak. What was it that I wasn't getting a feel for or asking? As a result I wrote about it in great detail in a *six minute free write* way, wrote some letters to the research part of myself and finally *finally* felt like I had found the missing part of the jigsaw! I feel as if I have a grasp on what I want my inquiry to entail!

> So – I shall continue to write letters to the different parts of myself, and most importantly will continue to ask *why?*

> (Claire Collins)

An MSc student was unable to frame his research question. I invited him to describe his proposed study in one sentence then and there, with no forethought. His immediate and stunning research question, began with Why. 'Why hadn't I thought of asking why before!', he gasped.

The question stem Why...? above interrogates the underpinning whys: the principles and values which should be the foundation of all academic enquiry. Thus the childlike endless query brings us to the foundation: Why is it important to undertake this study? Why is it helpful to mankind/society/culture?

Stephen

I am always struck by the very different reasons people want to publish, and this shows in the way they write. Some communicate their genuine passion for the subject matter; others want to pursue a particular social or ideological mission (such as gender equality); others publish for more strategic reasons such as the development of their career or their institution. All are justifiable answers to the question 'Why should I publish this?'

Knowing why I want to publish is not always a straightforward question to answer. When I retired from full-time academic work many of my colleagues assumed I would now devote more time to writing since, they believed, my writing was motivated by intellectual rather than career interests. However, I almost completely stopped writing and no longer saw myself as a 'writer', and now spend my time playing the piano and being a seriously involved grandparent. Sometimes, I think my own motives are the most difficult ones to ascertain with certainty: self-knowledge is not easy. That is why the kind of reflective questioning suggested above can be so useful.

Why an author wants to impart their passion and wisdom about a specific area tends also to get lost in the writing process, perhaps because writers fear a judge with a red pen will mark it down as too personal and insufficiently academic or critical. Anxiety about pleasing this non-existent teacher can prevent writers from communicating properly with their real reader. The received detached authorial voice of scholars, researchers and intellectuals is unemotional. Yet being able to read our own emotions, and make use of them, is an empowering process.

Stephen

The word 'critical' keeps cropping up. I think it's a really slippery concept to grasp, not helped by the fact that in everyday language 'critical' comes with all sorts of negative connotations of disapproval, opposition and even hostility. In most academic discourses, however, being 'critical' is seen as a *sine qua non* of academic debate and intellectual activity. But the difference between these two apparently opposing meanings may not quite so clear as I hope this anecdote will show.

Sally, a 'mature' PhD student in a fairly senior university position was researching university change, and I encouraged her to read broadly around the field. I suggested she read a UK Government committee report, commonly called 'The Dearing Report', an important document for Higher Education policy in UK.

Sally looked at me with some alarm when I suggested she write a critical commentary. Lord Dearing, she said, was a very eminent and knowledgeable gentleman and who was she – a mere PhD student – to criticise his report? There was then some discussion in which I felt we

(Continued)

(Continued)

may have clarified what I had in mind for her to write. Her co-supervisor and I both smiled at the student's naivety in confusing the everyday with the academic usage of the term 'critical'.

I began, however, to wonder how critical I and my colleagues really were. It seemed to me that in most fields of study there were 'key texts' which were invariably cited without critique. In the social sciences at that time Michel Foucault was one such writer. Experienced academics (as well as PhD students) whom I encountered seemed to view this author as also 'an eminent and knowledgeable gentleman'.

Amongst many papers published in academic journals in my field, it had become fashionable to adopt a 'Foucauldian perspective' as though the eminence of the academic himself was enough to make critique of his perspective unnecessary. I think it would not be too outrageous to suggest that the one thing that binds together the papers published by a particular journal is the group of key thinkers – the 'eminent gentlemen' – who are viewed by the journal's contributors to be beyond criticism. Perhaps, like the 'peers' in the House of Lords, 'peer review' has as much to do with establishing the club of 'eminent gentlemen' of the academic field as it does with intellectual acuity. (NB: my gendered use of language here is intentionally provocative.)

Such thoughts made me wonder if it really is possible to view *all* sources of knowledge critically. Don't some things just have to be accepted in order for enquiry to get off the ground? This question is too difficult to pursue just here, I think. But the question reminds me that the term 'critical' is a more problematic idea than is often assumed. For some, such as Habermas (1974), it denotes a thought-through philosophical and sociological position (as in 'critical theory'); for others an ideal for student engagement; for others merely a questioning approach. In relation to any paper I write, I find it useful to ask myself the question: upon whom (or what) am I exercising a critical perspective and what do I accept uncritically? That's never easy to answer, but the attempt to do so is well worth the struggle.

Belonging to a Critical Writing Community

Belonging to a supportive writing community can help writers find and develop confident critical lines of enquiry (see Aitchison and Lee, 2006). It can enhance confidence using authors' own voice, style and focus. An effective group can be as small as two, and can usefully be from different disciplines. The members develop shared ground rules, and decide to trust each other to be helpfully critical rather than just laudatory and encouraging, and are willing to give prime time to working with the others' writing.

Finding the right colleagues can seem trickier than it needs to be. Beginning by developing shared ground rules helps potential group members (or partners) perceive whether they are right for each other. Shared assumptions and values might be good, or might lead to lack of critical enquiry. Opposing ones could lead to perceiving things which have been taken for granted but not provide sufficient shared ground for the trusted respectful support required by critical engagement.

Group members can help each other learn how to improve and demystify writing by sharing their drafts with each other, offering positive criticism and sharing insight learned from their reading of the literature. They can create strategies for effective timetabling of dedicated writing time and reduction of time-wasting rituals (e.g. reading emails before starting to write), and support each other through blockages and lapses of confidence. They could even set up writing sanctuaries for themselves, predetermined periods of time for writing in the same house, part of the institution or even a hostelry (see Mewburn, 2011). And they can 'workshop' sections of each other's drafts, making helpfully critical suggestions for redrafting, drafting additional material or seeking a change of focus. For all these there are plenty of ideas and exercises in this book.

Each group member, as well as being caring and giving, and willing to use all their critical powers in the service of another, could also watch out for one who takes but gives little in return. I've only ever encountered one, but she sucked blood from the group, ultimately destroying it because we couldn't get rid of her, and could not work with her present. Had we been a formal group, I suppose the leader would have managed the situation. I learned a lot about trust and respect through that experience, and realised the absolute necessity for very clear boundaries, sad though that necessity might seem.

Academic writers might find it difficult to expose their writing in this way and ask for help, because it can be a competitive and secretive culture, rather than collaborative. Yet my experience of academic writers' retreats is that participants blossom after initial hesitance and anxiety. Creative writing (particularly poetry) has a culture of bravely and seriously critiquing each other's writing: it is part of the lifeblood of their writing and redrafting. Academic creative writing courses have made such groupings formal, a vital element of the curriculum for students of the novel, drama and poetry: such workshop opportunities need to become equally central for academic writing. Writing in an environment where there are other supportive writers present, or perhaps in another room in the same building, for example, can make it less lonely and isolated and a more pleasurable, motivating and productive experience. It too often feels 'cabined, cribbed, confined' (Shakespeare, *Macbeth*, 3. 4. 38).

My trusted first reader, as I think of Stephen in this role, is invaluable in my writing life. Since I have shared every draft publication with him, I have felt a confidence in my writing voice, and an additional ability to adapt that voice to suit different readers. He laughs at my clumsinesses and mistakes; we are a group of two: I read his, and also laugh with him. My besetting sin is being FAR too enthusiastic and making claims I can't substantiate, his is to be academically obtuse with abstractions and obfuscating sentences and paragraphs, and dreaded double negatives.

There are other tried and tested ways of gaining discussion and feedback on the content of draft manuscripts, such as presentation as conference papers: never write a conference paper, but present a draft publication. Sending a draft paper to a journal to see the reviewers' comments is, however, not a good way to gain formative feedback. Reviewers will suss poor drafts quickly and be understandably unwilling to give full critical attention.

Don't hesitate; take courage in both hands, and find a trusted, confidential first reader or group of readers. There is an Eastern saying that the boulder in the path is the path. The best route is to tackle the boulder itself, rather than seeking to get around it. Asking a trusted respected reader directly what they think of our writing, and responding positively to whatever they say, is doing just that.

Stephen

Not nearly enough emphasis is put upon the importance of this critical collegial relationship, I think. For PhD students, such a relationship should be an integral part of study, but sadly this is often not the case. As a supervisor I facilitated relationships between students in which they can be mutually supportive. But it's not always straightforward.

The trusted reader needs to share (or be prepared to share) the writer's interests to engage with their writing. But it is not helpful if their interests and perspectives are so closely aligned that they are unable to offer different and possibly conflicting interpretations. In the social sciences, where questions of social justice often underlie research, having a trusted reader who shares your perspective (say for gender equality or the rights of prisoners) can provide a valued sense of solidarity. On the other hand, it can also lead to mutual reinforcement which is uncritical and closes down real questioning. A relationship which is both supportive and offers critique is an immensely valuable intellectual asset.

PhD supervision itself can provide this function to some extent, but this is really rather different. However open and friendly the supervisor/student, it is a relationship of power in which the supervisor is expected to be critical towards the student's writing, but student critique of the supervisor's writing is much less common. As a consequence, the PhD student may respond defensively to criticism. Supervisors need to be gentle enough to overcome such defensiveness and encourage openness at the same time as offering important critical commentary.

How to Give and Receive Critical Feedback

Here are elements I've worked out are useful when reading and commenting on a colleague's draft:

- Before beginning to read at all, I like to find out what the other person hopes from my reading. On occasion I've made the mistake of spending ages doing a thorough edit, when what they wanted was an overview of whether the argument works.
- I ask for a printout double spaced, or at least space and a half, for easy reading, and to give space for scribbled notes (using any colour but red, the colour of the strict teacher's pen).
- Once I have some sense of their needs and wants in mind, I start by reading through to get a sense of the whole sweep. Then I note all the good things about it: starting by being positive will help the writer respond positively to my criticism. Even if the draft is in a real muddle, I always begin my response with the positive elements I can find. Then I can carefully word my suggestions for improvement (I don't even think of these as negative even then).
- Finally I write a paragraph summarising what I think the publication says and what I have taken from it. This is respectful, and can open up discussion about what they really meant, or helps to develop their argument. I tell them what I've noticed, and where I stopped focusing. Doing this I am not solving problems, but working out my own response as a reader: both positive and negative. Sometimes they discover they are saying all sorts of things they didn't realise they were, or failing to saying what they really intended to impart.
- Being specific is most useful to the writer; being vaguely supportive and encouraging is of no use at all. *Inspirational Writing* gives plenty of information about good writing, as well as suggestions for how to improve.
- We are not rewriting our colleague's publication, but helping them develop their thinking, or, if they've specifically requested it, offering editing advice.
- When the argument in the written paper seems less clear than I've remembered the author saying, I ask them to tell me again verbally, then suggest they write immediately what they said. This tends to feel harder than it is; often people have asked me to write it down for them, but of course I won't: it needs to be in their words.
- Taking a cue from good copy-editors can be useful. I had a fantastic one when I edited a regular section for a peer-reviewed journal. She always made her suggestions positive, even when she was pointing out errors: for example 'this instead? … ', 'repetition?' instead of 'that's rubbish!', or 'repetition!' I always accepted every one of her suggested revisions. A more recent book copy-editor substituted her own sections for mine, with no discussion (such as beginning a paragraph with 'However…'). Prejudiced against her suggestions, I reinstated my own grammar and phrasing: her work was a complete waste of time.
- If it is simply not possible to give the help the writer needs, then I've found it best to be completely honest and say so. I once couldn't make head nor tail of a piece by a European professor colleague, despite being certain it was extremely

erudite, entirely because of cultural and language differences. I spent some time, but had to send the draft back saying I found I had some block with it which I couldn't overcome, and so couldn't help in any way.

- Finally I try to listen to the advice I give others. We often tell other people things we should really be telling ourselves.

Now here are some ideas from my experience of reacting to a first reader's response to my draft:

- I try to read the response at a calm clear moment, unhurriedly and as unemotionally as possible. Or if it is verbal, I just listen and take notes without saying anything until the other person has said their fill. Then we go through discussing the notes.
- If their response is all negative, I ask for them to say the good points.
- If they just give a list of further reading to strengthen the argument or position, I feel this is a copout: they are not really engaging. So, I thank them and ask: but what did you think of what I said? It is my publication; it's not the role of the first reader to focus just upon what it does not include. That is merely thinking about what they would have written in my place.

Sharing ideas with others develops and extends them, for us as well as them. When the other person publishes material as a result of this discussion, it will inevitably be different from what I might write. Hoarding ideas for our own future publications will not be beneficial: we all know how well the proverbial miser did burying his gold.

Networking and seeking advice from experts

Social networking or other online contacts can be excellent ways of seeking support, advice or specific information, as well as the face-to-face discussions described above. Collegial and professional networks can be developed within disciplinary areas and beyond into interdisciplinary areas. Academic life is hedged tightly into disciplines; yet interdisciplinary elements within a study can bring them to life. Making use of contacts can inform research quickly and effectively: people, even important ones, rarely mind being asked and will generally do their best to advise or help.

Engaging with the wider community

Each academic publication is part of a wide community. The other elements of this community, the literature of the field, inform each new publication, providing its foundation. So every writing project involves researching the literature. This can be done constructively, respectfully of the writers we are reading, and imaginatively. I recently read in an instruction guide on academic writing, 'reading must be rigorous and systematic'. I scribbled in the margin 'oh dear, and then they'll write a boring paper!' Yet two pages later these authors contradict themselves and say, sensibly, how effective researchers read broadly and eclectically, often gaining inspiration from unexpected places or disciplines.

We read the literature for two main reasons: to set our work firmly within its field, and to extend and develop our own ideas. Lack of this clear location must be one of the major reasons for academic publications to be rejected by publishers and journal peer reviewers. Yet a mere parroting of the words of authoritative texts (Smith and Bloggs said ...) is another reason for rejection. A publication demonstrating the theories, ideas and finding of the author(s), while critically showing its place among similar and related publications, is likely to be accepted.

So, we trawl the literature (journals, books, other sources) for any research, studies, examination of theories, discussions which are at all similar to ours, or bring any interesting light to bear upon our research. We keep concise accurate notes including full reference to the work. A quote needs to be accurate down to the commas, and stored with full reference including page numberss.

A skill of reading a paper or book is to grasp the main plot of the argument and take a note of it, in my own words, succinctly and clearly. I skim the paper first to see if it is useful, then focus on the main argument and any concise relevant details. I try to note only these, knowing that if I write too much I won't bother to reread and make use of it.

Another strategy, and one I used for writing this book, is to turn down the corners of relevant pages, and scribble in the margin beside the interesting passage. I then reread to see if I still thought these were useful (quite a few weren't after all), and wrote a brief note on a sticky paper which then stuck out from the page for ready reference (these weren't library copies).

When I first started taking notes from my reading I didn't distinguish between my own reflections and ideas and those of the author. I had to work out a system for making this crystal clear, otherwise this muddle could have led to plagiarism or misrepresentation, both pretty bad sins in academic writing. In fact I'm dealing with this in this first draft of this chapter: I've written myself a note highlighted in red to sort out whether I am quoting this particular author, or what.

An enquiring attitude is essential to academic writing. It is one thing to know what this is, and quite another, however, to keep to it consistently. Gaining authority over our own writing at all times is likely to ensure this.

Don't just read: WRITE!

Here are activities that will help you move from thinking about writing, to actually doing it.

1 Write (preferably on paper) in a free-flow way with no specific subject, for *six minutes*, dumping whatever is in your mind onto the page. Do it every morning for at least a week. This is also a very effective way to begin every writing session (see above for full explanation and examples).

2 At the beginning of a writing session, without looking at any of your other material beforehand:

- Brainstorm or make a list, or jotting seemingly random notes, preferably away from your desk):

  o What do I now think I want to write about?

- Allow yourself to write as much as arrives at the end of the pencil, or as little.
- Read this list carefully, circle what seem to be the main points or themes, and then the subthemes or issues.
- Is there now anything else you'd like to add to these main and sub areas?
- Now look back at the brainstorm. Is there anything to which you have given surprising prominence? Is there anything you missed out?
- What does this tell you?

3 Make a list of questions to ask yourself, each beginning with Why …
Write a couple of sentences in response to each about the writing you are working on. Develop these sentences critically.

4 Write a letter to your research self. Write the reply (see above for more suggestions).

5 Stick a couple of pieces of A1 paper together end to end, using them lengthwise.

- Draw a line across the double page.
- Starting with childhood, put the names of people who've influenced you (and who have perhaps affected your writing) along the line, ending with the present day.
- Choose one: write about them in a way that seems appropriate to you, such as:

  o Describe a significant occasion with them, telling it as a story with as many details and description as occur to you.
  o Write them a letter and write their reply.

And READ some more:

Aitchison, C., Kamler, B. and Lee, A. (eds) (2010) *Publishing Pedagogies for the Doctorate and Beyond*. Abingdon, Oxon.: Routledge.

Grant, B. (2008) *Academic Writers' Retreats: A Facilitator's Guide*. Milperra, NSW: HERDSA.

Aitchison, C. and Guerin, C. (2014) *Writing Groups for Doctoral Education and Beyond: Innovations in Practice and Theory.* Abingdon, Oxon.: Routledge.
These three books have valuable information about writing groups and retreats (Aitchison et al. includes one chapter on the subject).

Carr, W. and Kemmis, S. (1986) *Becoming Critical.* Lewes: Falmer Press.
A well-thought-through account of what it is to be critical in an educational context, drawing on the work of the critical theorist J. Habermas.

Woodward-Kron, R. (2002) 'Critical analysis versus description? Examining the relationship in successful student writing', *Journal of English for Academic Purposes,* 1 (2): 121–44.
Although focused upon student writing, this study is as useful for academic writing for publication, and makes a valuable distinction between descriptive and critical functions in writing.

8

Write with Authority

The author has authority over their own writing: these two words come from the same root. This chapter explores how to establish this authority. The first route is to locate writing firmly within its field. The second is to take care of the implicitly expressed values, because nothing exposes a bogus intellectual more effectively than dodgy or inconsistent values. The third is completely different and is to tackle the damagingly negative internal terrorist, and find the helpful internal mentor. The fourth is how to draw readers authoritatively into the subject, enabling them to perceive and understand: this is a vital but simple tip directly from creative writing.

Seamus: Values are really important in my teaching, but is there a place for them in my research? Or are research values different from teaching ones? And how do I put them in? And how does all this fit in with the literature in the field?

Helena: I sit down to write and a voice in my head says 'You're useless. Who do you think you are that you can write like this?' And I freeze. I think that voice is right, and so I don't have the courage to explore what I think and have discovered. I hope this chapter gives me strategies to deal with this.

I think I'm afraid of the reader. Yet this book tells me they are on my side, that they really want to hear what I have to say. Can I believe this, and believe I am really engaging in conversation with them?

And can I use the experience of art again to enable me to understand how to write? We never boringly tell reviewers things in an artwork: we 'show' them; and we use narrative and metaphor to make the 'showing' more powerful. *Telling* a viewer stuff is not art.

Lee: I present my methods and results in detail. But I'm told that's not enough, that it's thin. How do I fatten it out? I know it's all clear, and that the problem is not my English. This chapter might help me refer to other literature better, to locate my work better alongside others.

Joseph: I'm used to thinking of power and conflict as social phenomena. In this chapter perhaps we'll get to grips with the battles that take place in our own heads.

Writing with authority is gaining respect for ourselves as writers, and trust that we can write. Publications are active in influencing and structuring the world as well as being a significant form of communication. They do a great deal more than just disseminate information, though of course they do this effectively as well. Successful academic writing is confident and authoritative in the way it communicates data, findings, theories and ideas to the reader. This confidence and sense of personal authority is essential, yet does not come naturally to every writer.

> Self confidence is the key to successful writing.
>
> (Academic writing course member)

I would add: self-respect, trust of the writing process and awareness that the author owns their own writing as well. These all add up to authority.

The Internal Terrorist and the Internal Mentor

We will start with the less well-known third route to confidence and authority in writing. Most writers have a destructive terrorist lodged inside them which attempts to sabotage confidence and sense of authority. The internal mentor's role is to assure the writer they certainly can do it and how. The terrorist creates such fear in writers that they can't access their store of knowledge and ability. It does what its name says: it not only blocks off confidence but also blocks movement, which is the lifeblood of communicative writing. Paying attention to the internal mentor and tackling the internal terrorist is an effective strategy against *writer's block* (also see Chapter 5). This writer's experience is, I think, very common:

> I can always hear a voice in my head whispering – What does she know about it? What an arrogant fool to think she does.
>
> (Academic writing course member)

Most writers have a self-destructive side (stronger in some than others) telling them their writing is rubbish, or worse. Many people think this negative voice is just themselves, not realising it is an element which can be counteracted. To disarm this internal terrorist, it can be useful to listen to it properly, when in a strong mood. And confront it, as this writer found:

> I have discovered my destructive inner terrorist can be separated from me, so I can tackle it – that is a huge liberation.
>
> (Academic writing course member)

Every writer also has a powerful advisory side. My internal mentor misses nothing, and is always there to support and advise me. Sometimes it's hard to hear this voice clearly, let alone allow it to support me. Valuing our diverse array of strengths, as well as attending properly to weaknesses, can help empower the former and go some way to developing positive strategies against the latter.

Listen to the Internal Mentor

The original *Mentor* was the goddess Athene, come in disguise to help Odysseus' young son search for his father who'd been lost at sea for ten years. Mentor's wisdom and judicial powers enabled a tangled mess of events to be sorted out, at least according to Homer's *Odyssey* over two thousand years ago. Once Odysseus was back home, and battling with the potential usurpers of his throne and marriage bed, Athene turned herself into a swallow to sit on the rafters where she could oversee everything, and offer advice.

> Athena kept on testing Odysseus and his gallant son,
>
> Putting their force and fighting heart to proof.
>
> For all the world like a swallow in their sight
>
> She flew on high to perch
>
> On the great hall's central roofbeam black with smoke.
>
> (Homer, *Odyssey*, 22. 248–52)

We can't all call on the help of a goddess, but can each find within ourselves a reliable mentor always available to offer advice and support. One writer here found this, the second initially had to come to terms with the tough advice of their mentor:

> I gained a supportive internal mentor I will connect with again.

I was shocked by the aggressiveness of my inner 'mentor'.

(Academic writing course members)

Any issue or problem can be given to the internal mentor in the research journal; I do it all the time. Sometimes when particularly stuck, I realise I've forgotten to ask, a simple but significant lapse of memory. People sometimes ask me 'should I do this or that?' 'Ask your writing, ask your Internal Mentor', I respond. One writer, with whom I had had this exchange by email, immediately replied saying 'Oh, thank you, I know what to do now'!

Once opened out in writing, several options generally come to light. It can seem like magic: but of course it's not. When things weigh heavy, it's often hard to see beyond them: thinking can go round and around in increasingly useless repetitive circles. Using writing constructively and privately in this way can help us leap over the walls of such stifling prisons. We can all have our own mentor available twenty-four hours a day, every day of the year, all our lives.

I have taken away a much kinder inside voice telling me what to do and how to do it.

(Academic writing course member)

A way of making contact with this mentor is to write letters or dialogues:

- Allow your internal terrorist to write you a letter, giving full rein to their criticisms.
- Now ask your internal mentor to respond.

Here is Bernadette Knewstubb's response from her Internal Mentor.

Hi Dette,

I think you are making this more complicated than it needs to be. Ok, there are two worlds, but the model shows all that.

What your lit review needs to do is to show where your ideas are from. Do I (as a reader) need to know Biggs was a constructivist? Not really, although yeah it's helpful to know that not all your studies are phenomenographic. So what *do* I need to know? ... Try going back to the postgraduate presentation you gave a couple of months ago – what references did you use then (those were clearly important)? How did you explain them to your Linguistics audience? That might be a good place to start. Cheers, Alison

(Bernadette Knewstubb)

Tackle the Internal Terrorist

Negatively critical forces are internalised at a very young age. People, particularly children, are surrounded by instructions: what to do, how to do it, with whom, when and where; all these often with no explanation of why. These know-alls (parents, grandparents, teachers, tutors, bosses, partners ...), instruct, advise and generally know better. Because these voices were strongly impressed on us when our memories were good, they have been carried forward into adult life.

Yet the only way to write well is to hold authority over what we say and how we say it.

Must, should, ought, shouldn't and *CAN'T* can be seen as the terrorist's wagging finger. Everyone has internalised a bullying voice to some extent. It nags inside the mind, saying we're no good, won't and can't succeed. We begin to believe we can't do it.

One of the secrets is to distinguish the voice of the terrorist as soon as it starts: it is so insistent and clever it sneaks under our defences. We all have a stronger voice in us which can say: *I WON'T listen to you! I WILL listen to my wiser internal guides!* Separating it off and giving it recognisable characteristics makes it possible to tackle.

Internal Terrorist Exercise

Coming to grips with this powerful but slippery aspect of myself needs specialist methods. One is to visualise it as a concrete thing or creature. Giving body to this invisible force can really help with tackling it. Winston Churchill famously had a Black Dog on his shoulder, for example. Black Dog is an ancient embodiment of this terror; inventing our own can be more powerful. Here is a simple, old and well-tried exercise.

1 Make a list, writing a phrase or sentence for each entry. If your internal terrorist were one of these, what would they be?

   i Animal
   ii Insect
   iii Sci fi or fantasy creature (invent one, but think of Tolkein, Harry Potter, Star Wars, etc.)
   iv Colour
   v Smell
   vi Drink
   vii Music
   viii Cleaning material or equipment

   ix Relative or someone else from your past

   x Make up your own categories

2 Write what it most commonly says to you.

3 Write your message to it.

Here is Ronan's internal terrorist:

1 A Lion, fierce but tameable

2 A bee, buzzing around in an annoying manner, but if you give it enough honey it will go away

3 The Terminator, cold, lifeless and inflexible

4 Blue, has their own stuff to deal with

5 Bad, the smell of fear

6 Whiskey, sharp, rough but with a distilled excellence

7 Wagner, pompous and overly tricksy

8 Always says: you lack critical depth!

9 Message to: go gently and try and be a bit positive. I can take the hard stuff then.

(Ronan Foley)

Locate the Work Authoritatively within the Field

This section might seem odd, given importance as it is here: of course all academics need to locate their work firmly in its field. Well yes, but many papers or books come for review with only a nod to the work of others, or with citations and quotes inserted inauthentically and unsatisfactorily. Or, perhaps even worse, unsubstantiated claims with no authoritative reference or indication that it is the author's own theory. Academic publications cover new material strongly related to work which others have researched and published. This is the ground from which the fresh views, ideas or dataset have sprung, and in which they are rooted. A new publication not only adds to existing research, but, perhaps more importantly, throws significant light on it.

Scholarly literature research is a trawl of the literature (journals, books, other sources) for any research, studies, examination of theories, discussions which relate at all to the current writing project or bring interesting light to bear upon it. When I'm developing ideas and connections, I scout around and read in depth others' ideas and theories to develop my own thinking, and to know how my own fits (or doesn't) with the rest of the field. I think of this process as scholarly research, an intellectual process; I don't like the pragmatic and technical term 'literature search' which sounds like a job for my computer without my aid. When I critically engage with others' positions in my writing, I give my work a place alongside theirs in the field.

We quote from literature with care. The authority of any text resides in *authors*' knowledge, analysis and their own argument. References to (or quotation from) the work of others cannot *replace* my own argument, nor my critical appreciation of what they have contributed and how I might add to it.

Academic writing takes a position of critical authority when it clearly and simply states a position, theory or argument, then cites, or quotes, using the words of others, either to back this up, or to offer an additional or alternative stand. Uncritically using the words of another in place of our own argument, especially beginning a section or paragraph (or even worse a whole paper or abstract) with a quotation, can be writing with lack of authority (e.g. 'As Snodgrass and Mellors (2015) state "…"').

> It was fantastic to realise that when I refer to other published authorities, they express *their* view; and *I* might disagree.
>
> (Academic writing course member)

Stephen

As a referee, I want to be engaged if I am to consider an article seriously for publication. Only then can I feel that the author and I are part of a wider conversation. The quotation of other sources is fine, but more is needed: I want to know their relevance. Referring to authors with different values, or who have taken a different tack, can help by showing me how in the wider conversation there are differences, conflicts and absences, not just agreement. When done well, I might want to talk with the author as soon as I've finished reading the paper. I don't need to be in agreement: I would rather recommend publication when I want to have a good argument with the author, than a proficient student in the field.

But take care! I have sometimes reviewed papers in which the author seems to be belligerent or aggressive in the lack of respect they show to those with whom they disagree. For me that's an immediate failure.

Similarly, PhD students in the social sciences have expressed themselves with hostility to views with which they disagree. The purpose of research supervision may then be to help the writer move from disrespect for other points of view to powerful and passionate argument. That will engage the reader.

Values

Awareness of values, and consonance between those which are espoused (stated) and those which are implicit within the methodology and methods of the research and the fabric of the text, are a measure of the integrity of that text. A publication is worthy of readers' respect because it has integrity when implicit values are demonstrated in the way the data were gathered, and these have coherence with those espoused and explained in the methodology section (for example). Within the academic publications I find most useful and informative to read, theory and values emerge naturally in the telling of the research story.

Furthermore, we all need to ask ourselves: Why do I want to say this? Why do I want you to hear this from me? Responding to this query can help us to reach our ethical and values basis for research and research writing. The other tin-opener questions (see p. 34) are practical (how, what, who, where, when) and straightforward to ask ourselves; questions beginning with WHY are too rarely asked of themselves by researchers and research writers. Being aware of the firm ethical and values base for each one of our publications is likely to ensure a committed, understanding readership.

Stephen

In everyday conversation the word 'academic' is often used pejoratively to indicate a way of thinking or view of no practical significance or of interest only to someone with their head in the clouds. That's unfortunate. In the social sciences (but not exclusively there) the best academic work often relates directly to values of social justice or humanity. What impresses me is when research reports are permeated by such values rather than just state value positions. I am then shown how these values were realised in the way subjects were selected, the interview process, the way their statements were interpreted, the respect that was given to their rights and so on. This has to be done with some care.

What is really offputting for a reviewer is when a writer's enthusiasm has blinded them to different points of view. A well-authored thesis or paper, like a good contribution to a conversation, may be explicit in its values and show them passionately, but also be ready to listen and converse with others who may not share them.

'Show' and 'Tell'

This is a real writer's tip. Accurate well-chosen and expressed details convey material far more powerfully and authoritatively than a statement about that scene or event. Memorable well-argued writing relies on its concrete material (data and examples) to give a spark to the whole publication. 'Yes!' the reader murmurs as they read, avidly turning the page, then after the conclusion they continue musing, allowing it into a dynamic relationship with their current research and writing.

An infuriating 'tell' in academic writing is 'I would argue that ... '. When I read a paragraph beginning thus, I just want to shout at the writer: well get on and argue it, don't give me a provisional personal statement. Stories, in the form of anecdotes or case studies, and metaphors are classic ways of 'showing' graphically in writing.

Stories

Anecdotal examples are generally included in texts to give details in the form of narrative. Humans learn from stories because we pay attention and remember information embedded in narrative. A strong element of narrative is the way the detail carries the story forward. A simple example is the way I am encouraged to want to know what's happening in a room where *the fire cast its ruddy glow over the young man curled on the hearthrug*. Whereas, I'm not in the least bothered to continue reading about events where *the fire made the room feel warm and cosy*. In the former sentence the fire, young man, and rug are all physical details which conjure up warmth and cosyness far more powerfully than in the latter sentence where these abstractions leave us cold. In the latter the writer has *told* me how the room feels; in the former I infer how it feels from the sensual details: the writer has *shown* me.

Metaphor

Metaphor is our standard human way of converting abstract to concrete to increase the power and accessibility of whatever is being described or explained. All speech and writing is stuffed full of metaphors: it is our standard way of making otherwise indigestible abstractions comprehensible and memorable. 'New research in the social and cognitive sciences makes it increasingly plain that metaphorical thinking influences our attitudes, beliefs, and actions in surprising, hidden and often oddball ways' (Geary, 2011: 3). And this most certainly includes academic thinking and writing. Geary continues:

> ... metaphor slips a pin into the quotidian ... By mixing the foreign with the familiar, the marvellous with the mundane, metaphor makes the world sting and tingle. Though we encounter metaphor every day, we typically fail to recognise it. Its influence is profound but takes place mostly outside our conscious awareness. (p. 4)

Most academic writers use metaphor 'outside [their] conscious awareness'; becoming aware of our use of it, and wielding it consciously, really can make academic writing 'sting and tingle' readers. Listen to science writer Deborah Blum:

> I've compared carbon monoxide [in the human blood] to 'a chemical thug' that 'muscles' oxygen out of the way and takes its place. Obviously, it's not quite that cinematic. But it allows me to create a clear image in a reader's mind of a chemistry-based process and I hope, a vivid one. (Blum, 2013)

We rarely notice metaphors: when I asked a group of doctors to give me an example of metaphor, they looked completely blank as if this idea is new to them, despite having perhaps been helped to understand the severity of a symptom that morning by hearing how a patient's throat was *on fire*. I felt they thought 'we're scientists, we don't know about such things', yet metaphor is central to scientific understanding. Bernadette Knewstubb used a story to explain complex abstract theory; the story is itself an extended metaphor:

A simple story with complex perspectives

> In the country where the kitset [for my new desk] was prepared, someone who speaks a completely different language had been given the task of teaching how to build the desk in a specific way. Because of potential language differences, step-by-step diagrams of parts and the relationships between them were provided, together with bits of laminated chipboard, nails, screws and other things. I dutifully followed the instructions, cursing when I couldn't see which type of bolt a particular diagram was referring to. At times I wanted to throw away the piece of paper and work it out by myself, deciding which bits would fit most logically where. However, I persevered, knowing that the person who had drawn the diagram knew what needed to be done, and that the diagram was my unknown teacher's way of communicating with me. Eventually I finished and stood back and looked proudly at the desk which I had learned to make, and at which I now sit, writing the introduction to my thesis. I begin with this story to draw attention to some of the different and complex questions which come into focus in this thesis, and to illustrate some of the ways in which disciplinarity affects the questions we ask, and the answers we find. ...

(Bernadette Knewstubb)

Erika Mansnerus uses original metaphor, narrative and other *showing* methods in her draft book about epidemiological modelling. Here are two separate extracts. In the first paragraph she uses the metaphors *victories; loud narratives, the silent ones whisper; natural habitat; buried; give birth*. In the second paragraph she uses very straightforward personal terms and constructions to draw the reader in, for example 'What will happen to us?' In the third, she brings the abstract and complex nature of epidemiological modelling alive with 'Let me reflect ...'. The draft book title is *Lives of Models: How Mathematical Techniques Keep Us Healthy*, a graphically descriptive use of metaphor (Erika is a non-native English speaker).

> Time and again we are challenged by new emerging infections and witness their victories amongst us. When the A/H1N1 'Swine flu' outbreak hit the headlines in 2009, we learnt of its rapid spread from country to country, how many people became severely ill and how many died. Along with these loud narratives, the silent ones whisper worries of common childhood infections. All these stories share something in common: They voice concerns, demand changes, and respond to policy calls. They reach beyond the natural habitat of scientific journals, where their findings may be buried and forgotten. The emergence of mathematical techniques in epidemiology give birth to these stories, and they are told to keep us healthy ...
>
> ... When a pandemic occurs and affects people across the globe, its rapid development increases the need to know, predict, anticipate and guess. On individual level, questions concerning personal health and well-being arise. What will happen to us? How does this affect me? What can I do to protect myself and my family? In cases like these, one's own ignorance in the face of the unpredictable nature of the pandemic itself is particularly hard to tolerate.
>
> Let me reflect on two personal experiences that capture the difficulty of accepting the uncertainties concerning a pandemic. When the number of confirmed cases of (H1N1) v influenza rose rapidly in mid July, 2009 in the UK, the media reached out to researchers who might shed some light on the story ...
>
> (Erika Mansnerus)

Metaphors can, however, have negative impact, especially when used unwittingly. There are many types or families of metaphor prevalent in our culture, so much so that we aren't always conscious of them (the market, ballgames). I try to check the metaphorical content of my writing to ensure they are consonant with my own values, and the ethical foundation of my research. There are some families of metaphors I avoid using. In medicine, for example, war metaphors have been standard for some time (she lost her battle with cancer). And the body and mind as machine also (writing exercises are 'tools'; the brain as computer). In many aspects of our lives we seem to be for sale in a permanent marketplace, we are customers instead of students, hospital patients or train passengers.

'Telling' as bullying

A further misuse of *telling* is when academic or PhD authors try to impose an opinion on their reader. I feel irritated and bullied by, for example, 'It is important that …'. I don't want to be told this is important; I want to work out its importance for myself from the writer's authoritative evidence. This is a lazy construction with 'it' being a spurious authority the writer is hiding behind.

Academic writing does have to include some *told* theory argument or ideas, unlike fiction or poetry. Subtly positioned narrated examples, metaphors and data detail will leaven this dry abstract writing and carry the reader into comprehension and interest. The *told* theory also needs to follow a clear narrative line.

Having gained respect for ourselves as writers with something to communicate to specific readers, next it's time to turn to finding the most appropriate publication.

 Don't just read: WRITE!

Here are activities that will help you move from thinking about writing, to actually doing it.

1 Write (preferably on paper) in a free-flow way with no specific subject, for *six minutes*, dumping whatever is in your mind onto the page. Do it every morning for at least a week. This is also a very effective way to begin every writing session (see above for full explanation and examples).
2 Respond to this question with a list, or a piece of reflective prose:
   Why do I want to write what I'm currently writing?
3 Make a list, writing a phrase or sentence for each entry. If your internal mentor were one of these, what or who would they be?

   • An animal
   • A plant of any sort
   • A food or drink
   • A relative or someone else from your past
   • Make up your own categories

   Describe her/him/it in more detail, using ideas from your list (see above for much more information).
4 Make up the kindest most helpful knowledgeable person or being you can imagine. Give her/him/it a name, but not the name of a real person you know. This only really

   (Continued)

(Continued)

works if you invent someone or something, or use an off-the-peg one like Goddess Athene.

- This is your *internal mentor*. Write her/him/it a letter asking for advice or help with a specific problem or issue.
- Write the reply, which might be lengthy. Continue the dialogue or letters if you wish. This doesn't always work the first time; if so, just leave it for a while and have a go another time.

5 Make a list, writing a phrase or sentence for each entry.

- If your *internal terrorist* were one of these, what or who would they be (see above for a full list of categories you can use, or use the list as in 3 above)?
- Now respond to this next list. How does your internal terrorist:

    o Walk and move?
    o Communicate with you?
    o Live with you (like the dog lived on Churchill's back)?
    o Attack you, and when?
    o Remind you of someone?
    o Make its presence felt normally?

- Write a dialogue or set of letters to and from your *internal terrorist*.

6 List critical things you say to yourself in your mind; make the list as long as you can, up to twenty items if possible (fifty even better). Try to be honest, remembering NO ONE else need ever read this. And don't be afraid to repeat yourself as often as you like. The items you repeat are the vital ones. Think specifically of what you find difficult: what are the words that come with lack of confidence, fear, or anxiety?

- Now list all the things you tell yourself you should, ought, must do. All these are probably spoken in the voice of your *internal terrorist*.
- Pick one from your lists. Write in a *six minute dump* way about it; this might be:

    o the critical voice given full rein to shout and rant onto the page: safely now because you know you are learning to be proof against its bullying;
    o a pouring out of thoughts and feelings in a reflective, possibly rather helpfully disorganised way;
    o an account of an appropriate event, including as many details as occur to you, as fully as you can.

- Imagine your *internal terrorist* speaking to you in the voice of the animal/thing/ however you depicted it in response to 5 above.

7 Write a dialogue between your internal mentor and your internal terrorist. Give them full rein to say what they both feel and think of each other and you.

Be gentle with yourself. Make sure you end with the voice of the internal mentor.

8   Look through a piece of your writing which you feel is not quite right, preferably unpublished. Find places where you have *told* the reader material which you could more effectively *show* them. Rewrite *showing* the reader. This might take some practice, but it's well worth working at (see above for a full explanation and examples of this useful process).

9   A values exercise:

1   Think of an important procedure or element in your research.
2   Write in response to: 'Why do I do this?'
3   Now ask Why? of your response to 2.
4   Now ask Why? of your response to 3.
5   Continue like this, until you reach a response which seems to you to be axiomatic (meaning no further justification is necessary or possible). For example, one chain might lead to 'because I want to seek the truth', or it might end up 'because I want to benefit humanity'. These are both values. And they have different implications for research (see above for more about values).

And READ some more:

Booker, C. (2004) *The Seven Basic Plots: Why we Tell Stories*. London: Continuum.
Written by the founding editor of the satirical magazine *Private Eye*, this substantial book goes into some depth, drawing upon a wide range of illustrations, to explore the basic plots that underlie all stories. It is based upon a Jungian approach to psychology which shows why narrative is so important in our lives.

Geary, J. (2011) *I is an Other: The Secret Life of Metaphor and How it Shapes the Way we See the World*. New York: Harper Collins Perennial.
Grasping the use of metaphor might be a royal road to illuminative academic writing, but we need a guide to help us do so. Lucid and readable, yet thorough and reliable, this book is just such a guide.

Lakoff, G. and Johnson, M. (1980) *Metaphors we Live by*. Chicago, IL: University of Chicago Press.
Drawing upon research in semantics, the focus of the book is the conceptual structures that govern the way we live. The authors' premise is that these conceptual structures, although generally present only on a subconscious level, can be explored through the medium of language. Such metaphors are found widely in academic writing, often communicating unintended meanings.

Nash, R. (2004) *Liberating Scholarly Writing: The Power of Personal Narrative*. New York: Teachers College Press.
Nash argues for the validity of an exciting, alternative approach to doing scholarly writing which he calls the 'scholarly personal narrative' (SPN). It offers tips and guidelines for writing an SPN. Although aimed at students, useful also to experienced academics.

9

Where to Publish?

A significant element of working out who my reader is and what specifically they want to know, is finding the appropriate publication, or choosing the doctoral examiners carefully.

Seamus: Now I'm getting the hang of it, and think I can join the community of published writers. I hope this chapter can help me to be clearer about what bit of that community is for me: what kind of publication. I hadn't thought before that the choice was mine: it's like there are lots of parties around: which one do I want to join?

I found writing a letter to my reader so useful to help me gain perspective on what I want to say, and having grasped that method, the letter to my Internal Mentor was really quite easy to get into and helpful.

Helena: Help! My supervisor has just said I should start publishing in journals. Where do I start? With a peer-reviewed journal (gulp), professional article, book chapter, book review? Or should I wait and rewrite my finished thesis as a book, and how would I do that anyway? I really took in how important it is to respect myself as a writer and to trust the processes of writing, but it's easier said than done!

Lee: The head of my research centre says I should write up my PhD into a book. It is very long. What should I cut?

Joseph: I sent my papers to the most prestigious journals, I know which ones they are, but they all rejected them. What's wrong? Am I being too ambitious? Stephen said journal editors don't just respond well to good theory, argument, ideas, solid methods and data; they respond positively to well-written papers, and negatively to badly written ones. Is this a hard lesson for me?

What are the Options?

In *Inspirational Writing* we use the generic term 'publication': however, the specific publication makes significant difference to how I write. Peer-reviewed papers, books, thesis into book, book chapters, doctoral theses vary according to discipline, in how much they count in academic review processes. Generally peer-reviewed academic papers come out top, though certain books might be considered equally important in some. There's a big distinction between books: textbooks for example, especially undergraduate ones, only count in that they can be good money earners; they can even be looked down on in academic circles. There are advantages of books over papers: a book is longer and so gives more scope to develop ideas and theories. Even long peer-reviewed journal papers might have strong editorial control exerted over them to keep the journal consistent. Book publishers rarely if ever seek such control, in my experience.

Chapters in books can help include academics in a debate, if the editor and other authors are reputable members of a community. Though I have heard of unwarranted editorial control, resulting in inauthentic, unauthoritative chapters, unsatisfactory to both writers and readers. Many edited books are conference paper compilations, of value to a limited specialist readership and can be an excellent first-time publication for, say, PhD students.

Turning a doctoral thesis into a book is a separate subject to be taken very seriously: there are too many around which are traps for the unwary reader. They look absolutely fascinating on first browse, but prove deadly dull because the author hasn't known how to address a book reader instead of doctoral supervisor or examiner. One postdoctoral fellow I'm helping has been advised by her book publisher to use a journalistic style, a bid to help the author see the kind of changes they feel are necessary.

Non-native English speakers have additional problems selecting where and how to publish. Whether they live and work in Anglophone countries or not, they are under pressure to publish in English to communicate with a wider readership, and advance their careers. English is the language of well over half of all scientific and social science journals, and their number is increasing (Lillis and Curry, 2010). Writing in a second language is a struggle, especially when that language is riddled with jargon. Since the dominance of English is perceived as inevitable and the language itself as transparent, the problems of non-English speakers are on the whole invisible (Canagarajah, 2002).

Remuneration for the tremendous amount of time and energy gobbled by academic writing is for most people restricted to possible promotion and job satisfaction; it is of course a more or less required element of normal academic work, or being a faculty member. Some universities and governments, however, do now reward financially on publication, particularly those which are peer-reviewed. It is possible this will adversely affect the quality and range of subjects researched and written about (Aitchison et al., 2013).

Peer-Reviewed Journals

How to choose? Having a look at example papers from the most appropriate-seeming journals, ones I already read to develop my own work, is a start. Peer reviewers only look favourably on papers which address subjects, and are couched in language, appropriate to their journal. Here are some strategies:

- Select from ones I read myself and find valuable and enjoyable.
- Choose a paper or two from each; study what subjects they cover, and how authors address the issues.
- Pay attention to the way they are written and how the writers address their readers: to do this I have to think beyond the content to the particular voice and style.
- Focus on the particular way the authors use language.

Stephen

When I review an article which makes no reference to anything published in the journal to which it is submitted, I wonder whether this is the right journal for it.

Rejection letters commonly include the advice to submit the article to a different journal. At its best, an academic journal can be seen as a conversation in which you are wishing to take part. To enter a real conversation without reference to what anyone has said is impolite if not disrespectful. So you need to be aware that your concerns have a place in the journal's dialogues. I think it is even worth going out of your way to make links between what you have to say and what others who have written for the journal have said.

Peer-Reviewed or Professional Journal?

Peer-reviewed journals require academic rigour and tone of voice, a professional journal needs language and information accessible to non-academics. A peer-reviewed journal paper will probably rate in academic review processes, whereas one in a professional journal almost will certainly not. An academic peer-reviewed paper is for colleagues to learn about our research and theories, and include them in the academic field. A professional article is for professionals to learn from our experience to develop their practice.

I have often followed up a peer-reviewed paper with a professional one on the same subject, but written in a lighter, more conversational, jargon-free voice, and with different examples and quotes. This allows me to enter my work into the canon of academic and intellectual thought in that area, and then to influence professionals in how they undertake specific areas of their practice. Following such publications I then receive feedback in the form of my theories and data being developed by other academics in their own research, and reports of how professional practice has been influenced, and how they have, also in turn, developed my practice as I reported it.

Books

Book writing involves a greater personal relationship with the publisher, generally a commissioning editor and her or his team, than does journal paper writing. Here, very simply, are my steps.

1 Before I have written much of the book I seek a publisher. This might be straightforward because I've been asked to write a book within a series: such series are generally edited by a senior academic whose role is to support the publisher in selecting and assessing new proposals. Or I perhaps wish to stay with a publisher with whom I have a good relationship, as is the case with SAGE. In both these latter cases I move straight to 5.
2 I select appropriate publishers in a similar way to journals (see above); I already know what kinds of texts they publish because I have used them in my work (whether for reference or textbooks for teaching, depending on the kind of book I am writing).
3 I look at publishers' websites, and make sure they are international.
4 I then make personal (email) contact with the appropriate editor, describing my proposed book in a few sentences.
5 If the editor responds positively she or he sends me proposal guidelines (also available on website).
6 Writing a book proposal takes some time, and is well worth the effort. It gives the publisher essential information, and demonstrates that I can write and set out text well and logically. I only send to one publisher; it wastes their time to send to more than one, and they might well know about me doing this, and both reject me. Writing a book proposal forces me to clarify for myself:

   a why I want to write this particular book
   b what I want to write
   c for whom I want to write it: specifically
   d what the competing titles are (list of published books with descriptions of their similarities and dissimilarities to mine)
   e how I want to write it: detailed chapter list for example
   f when I can complete the MS by (this date has to be adhered to; I always add three months to my sensible estimate because Phase 3 can take so long)
   g whether this is the right publisher for me.

7 A book proposal is a significant task. What I write for 6a–c is the foundation of my later marketing blurb. 6d–f really help me once I get stuck into writing. I need to get 6g right, because my publisher will support me to write what I want to write, and for the appropriate readership.

8 Publishers generally require one or two sample chapters. It's worth completing these carefully, proving to my future editor that I can write and manage the processes of writing.

9 Publishers then send the material out to peer reviewers, who respond. *Inspirational Writing*'s reviewers suggested plenty of example material.

10 If my chosen publisher rejects my proposal, that means they are not right for me, and I continue my search. It is disheartening, but we all know so many stories of incredibly successful books turned down initially.

11 If the publisher sends a contract, I study it carefully, perhaps even seek the support of an organisation such as the Society of Authors. For this book my publisher and I renegotiated royalty rates and submission date.

12 Publisher/editor, their assistant, copy-editors, proof readers, copyright advisers, marketing department, etc. then all support me through writing, MS preparation, cover choice, marketing, etc.

Rewriting a Doctoral Thesis as a Book

Now this is much more vital and tricky than many people imagine. A lengthy piece of academic writing has satisfied senior academics in the same field as being worthy of one of the highest degrees in the world; can it be bettered? Yes. Those doctoral examiners are an entirely different readership to a book or academic paper reader, looking for very different merits.

Attaining a doctorate indicates we have made a significant contribution to knowledge, and are sufficiently competent as scholars to demonstrate this. Examiners need to know exactly how this contribution was made.

Book readers on the other hand are primarily interested in what knowledge we possess and can therefore give them, and only secondarily in how we gained it. So many academic books are disappointingly turgid and often unreadable because authors leave the emphasis as it was for the thesis: I do not want to know all the ins and outs of their methodology, methods, data and so on. I want to skip to the chase and know about what they found, and I want some anecdotes and examples, etc., which they might have omitted from their thesis as inappropriate.

When I read a book, I want the author to know, and demonstrate that they know, that I am a peer interested in developing my own thinking and ideas and their grounding in the field, not an examiner. For example, I want to hear a succinct account of theory and research, not drown in data and references. I've just peer-reviewed a fascinating book proposal: the author, however, proposed writing 130,000 words; a doorstop not for reading in bed or the bath. My main recommendation was that the author should cut this to no more than 80,000 words and ensure he was addressing a book readership and not his PhD examiners for a second time round. 'If in doubt put it IN to a thesis'; 'if in doubt leave it OUT of a book'.

Taking a good break after completing the thesis can give critical distance, and enable strength and enthusiasm to be regained: completing a doctoral thesis can be draining. Attempting to work on the thesis before this exhaustion has passed might well be counter-productive, creating writing only fit for the delete button. We're not good at allowing space between undertakings or phases of life in our culture, but doing so certainly pays dividends.

Stephen

A common perception is that PhD theses should be written in an 'academic style' whereas a book should be written in a 'journalistic style'. I rewrote my research thesis as a book (1984) and, when it was reviewed in a national paper, the reviewer, an experienced and well-published researcher, poo-pooed its 'journalistic style' as being inappropriate to serious research. It was subsequently glowingly rereviewed by a more eminent academic: even accomplished academics have very different views about style. It is so important to find your own voice and not attempt to mimic a way of writing that is not yours. When I examine a PhD thesis I am not looking for a different style from a book. I wonder whether Gillie's observation (with which I agree), that PhD theses subsequently published as books are often dull, may be because they were dull theses in the first place: many are. The particular academic pressures under which PhD students (and possibly their supervisors) work does not always encourage an engaging style.

Chapter in an edited book

The initial readers of these are book editors, who are likely to be peers. Writing such a chapter can be wonderful or terrible, depending on how the editors perceive their role. Edited books need some sort of coherence, to tell a story, not be a bag of odds and ends. Some editors seek to control authors, however, wishing for uniformity throughout the book, squashing out authorial voices and interest: one wonders why they don't just write a single-author book (publishers far prefer them after all).

A good editor welcomes the range and depth brought by different voices, and supports authors to write at their best yet still remaining within the brief of the book as a whole. One of my students experienced a seriously controlling book editor. But she stuck out for what she wanted to say and how:

the editor ultimately wanted her contribution sufficiently to back down and accept her rewritten submission. She came out of the tussle with a chapter considerably strengthened by her rewriting; he gained a strong chapter with individual voice and focus.

Stephen

I think the editor/contributor relationship needs to be handled with care. Several acquaintances have fallen out badly over the way one colleague (editor) sought to exercise control over another (contributor), or the way in which contributors refused to recognise editors' requirements.

Editing a book

Editing a book is a whole different territory: hugely time-consuming, potentially massively frustrating but also utterly rewarding. Editing others' work is frustrating because potential authors send material late, first draft only, with inappropriate content or the voice completely wrong. Many a time I've enunciated clearly (or so I thought) what the book needed, only to be sent wildly out of place stuff. Editing can also be wonderfully rewarding, a way for new writers to learn to be authors. Supporting beginners to understand book and publishers' wants and needs can be teaching at its best. I am very proud of some of my edited books, and feel pleased at having given significant support to some chapter authors.

Book Review

Reviews share vital information, and often the reviewer's views. Giving the book's main message succinctly and enticingly can be exacting, searching for the good points can sometimes be tricky. A review starts with the main message, moves onto more detail about why and how the book is useful or interesting. It might end with some negative points, if there are any. There is often a quote along the way, to give a flavour of the book author's voice. I used to love writing reviews, seeing it as a game to communicate effectively with readers briefly (straight reviews rather than review articles, which are much longer). Two authors told me I was the only one to get to the heart of their book, making the whole process rewarding. I learned early to refuse to review publications negatively, having made the mistake of pointing out glaring ethical faults in a book's methodology. Although my analysis was accurate, the fallout with the author was not worth it: I kept my counsel on problem books after that, refusing to review them. When reviewing, I

- read the book through, as an ordinary reader;
- immediately write my initial impressions, using *six minute* type reflective writing (Phase 1);
- list the main thesis and points;
- reread quickly to check and develop these thoughts;
- write a draft, as if a letter to the reader;
- seek a/some characteristic quotes;
- give it a rest for a while;
- reread, redraft, edit (Phases 2, 3);
- ensure I've included accurate details, including ISBN number, number of pages, price.

Joint Authorship

Collaborating in writing has great advantages and disadvantages. In the sciences teamwork and joint authorship are quite common, less so in social sciences, and less again in the arts.

Sharing authorship can create opportunities for critical discussion; good co-authors learn from each other, though of course the relationship sadly can sometimes turn sour. I have had excellent experiences where the best ideas were undoubtedly my colleagues'. I have had tough experiences where I have held a team together and done nearly all the work. I have had a disappointing experience where one team member was a drone and I didn't realise how little work he'd done until after publication. One disastrous experience was of time-consuming initial phone and email discussions which led nowhere, because when I said we should start writing, the biggest mouthed suddenly didn't have time.

Co-authors bring different knowledge, skills and experience which can lead to stress and even resentment. One author might do less work, but perhaps the publication would never have happened if it was not for her experience of publishing, for example.

Co-authors do need to have clear respectful and trusting agreements. I suggest they

- Read carefully what each other has written before starting on their own contribution.
- Be clear what authority they have to change (or even suggest deleting) elements of others' writing.
- Know how quickly each is expected to return the next draft.
- Feel the paper is theirs while working on it.
- Respect others' sense that some writing is redundant or unnecessary, and trust their judgement. Once a co-author demanded I omit a section with which I was pleased: it became a centre piece of a later publication; I'm still pleased with it and have had good feedback.

111

There are many ways of co-authoring. I have only done it by each writing agreed sections, then each reading the whole critically and sharing the redrafting and editing stages. Some write together at one computer (this must be slow); some plan together and then one writes, and the other redrafts and edits. With scientific projects with a team of co-authors, the tasks might be allocated according to skill and knowledge: one writing up the methods, and another handling the statistics perhaps, and so on.

Jointly authored work might not advance the career of all the authors. My professorial head of department insisted his name be first on a paper about my first research project, which I had written. I fear this is the experience of many early stage researchers. Whatever the collaboration strategy, co-authoring is time-consuming and requires self-discipline, patience, trust and respect.

Journal papers, books and theses all have required forms. These are discussed in the next chapters, as well as significant issues of coherence and structure. Addressing these will help our publications communicate well with the right readers.

 Don't just read: WRITE!

Here are activities that will help you move from thinking about writing, to actually doing it.

1 Write (preferably on paper) in a free-flow way with no specific subject, for *six minutes*, dumping whatever is in your mind onto the page. Do it every morning for at least a week. This is also a very effective way to begin every writing session (see above for full explanation and examples).

2 Write a letter to your chosen publisher or journal editor; tell them why they should accept it.
Write their reply. Do not post these letters!

3 Write a review (as if a book review) of the publication you are working on, as if it were finished and published.

4 Write a 500–1000 word piece about your research for a section of the national press devoted to higher education issues. Or for a popular magazine: choose a specific one (e.g. your local paper).

5 Draw an image as an illustration for your paper.

6 Share and discuss it with a trusted colleague you can have a good light conversation with (NOT someone stuffy who might say, 'why are you doing this?').

And READ some more:

Aitchison, C., Kamler, B. and Lee, A. (eds) (2010) *Publishing Pedagogies for the Doctorate and Beyond*. Abingdon, Oxon.: Routledge.
This accessible book includes chapters on PhDs by publication, mentoring doctoral students towards publication and editing a special issue of a journal: this latter is not included in *Inspirational Writing*, and might be of value to readers.

Canagarajah, A. Suresh (2002) *A Geopolitics of Academic Writing*. Pittsburgh: University of Pittsburgh Press.
This book critically examines the politics of academic writing and shows how scholarly publishing practices and principles lead to inequalities in the way academic knowledge is constructed and legitimised. It argues that the dominance of the broad Western conventions governing academic writing has the effect of marginalising the knowledge of Third World communities.

Doctoral Writing Special Interest Group: http://doctoralwriting.wordpress.com (accessed September 2013).
An insightful blog about the doctoral research and writing process, written and edited by Australian and New Zealand academics Cally Guerin, Claire Aitchison, Inger Mewburn and Susan Carter.

Lillis, T. and Curry, M. (2010) *Academic Writing in a Global Context: The Politics and Practices of Publishing in English (Literacies)*. Abingdon, Oxon.: Routledge.
This examines the impact of the growing dominance of English on academic writing for publication globally. It explores the ways in which the global status attributed to English is impacting on the lives and practices of multilingual scholars working in contexts where English is not the official language of communication and throws into relief the politics surrounding academic publishing.

Paltridge, B. and Starfield, S. (2007). *Thesis and Dissertation Writing in a Second Language: A Handbook for Supervisors*. London: Routledge.
This book covers a vital area which needed this specialist attention.

10

Coherence and Unity

Here we explain how to create a coherent publication through informative structure and pacing. A good narrative flow, effective beginnings and endings, and consistency throughout are all essential.

Seamus: My lectures and seminars always have a clear structure and flow, carrying the students through from what they know to what is new to them. How do I achieve that flow in writing a paper? I think my best lectures are really just a good story, and I always keep to the point or the students would start texting on their mobile phones (cell phones). But what's a good sort of story, with consistency and flow, for a research paper?

Helena: My supervisor says it's good I'm really expressing myself, and communicating better. But what's not great is that it's all over the place! It's as though I have become a beginner all over again: I know very well how to construct narrative in a picture, and hold the viewer. And I can write *about* pictures with narrative flow. I need to transfer this skill to academic writing, and learn about narrative structure in writing, and how to begin and how to end, and how to hold readers' attention. I'd like some advice from this chapter about the building blocks of academic writing – what are essential ingredients (mixing up my metaphors terribly here!)?

Lee: My first reader (thank you *Inspirational Writing*, I really need her) says my writing still does not say all it can. She says it is still thin and dry and reads all jerky and disconnected, and my introduction and conclusion are weak. I need help on structure from this chapter, but I'm very unclear how 'narrative' can help me.

Joseph: It's only just occurred to me: I had assumed that, just because I could follow the sequencing of my own ideas, that it would all be clear to the reader. What I need from this chapter is how to make sure that the structure of this sequence is clear to the reader.

Academic writers invite readers to accompany them on a dynamic journey. Being able to do this is a significant development from being just a researcher writing up, to becoming a writer. Those who think of writing as static, an arrangement of marks on a page, produce workmanlike pieces of reportage which drop out of readers' memories.

Draw the Reader in; Keep Them Interested

Readers want to be drawn into a publication, carried along by its logical flow, the narrative, from the opening enticing paragraph to the fascinating conclusion. This is as true for scientific and technical publications as it is for the arts and social sciences. Readers are all human, whatever their discipline; and a good structure with narrative flow is what makes a paper not only readable but memorable. Most humans understand and remember in story form, not computer-like data. Even a medical drug trial, for example, can be told as a story with narrative interest, enabling readers to follow and remember.

Stephen

When Gillie first told me her ideas about narrative and writing I remember thinking that this is all very well for 'creative' writers of 'literature' or perhaps for research in the arts and humanities. But I didn't see its relevance to, say, mathematics.

Then I recalled Euclidean geometry, which is concerned with proving such interesting things as the sum of the angles in a triangle or the area of a parallelogram. The required proof was strictly logical, a series of steps in a strictly ordered fashion, ending with 'Q.E.D.' (*quod erat demonstrandum*, or 'that which was to be proved'). Much later, when I taught 9 year olds in a primary school, I realised that the satisfaction they felt when they ended their story with 'and they all lived happily ever after', was rather like mine when I wrote Q.E.D. at the end of the proof. Their story inevitably involved some problem which they resolved and so the characters could indeed now live happily ever after. Both geometrical proof and story writing involve a problem which has to be solved.

It now seems to me that narrative is as fundamental to logical (or scientific) thinking as it is to artistic. The difference is just that in logical or scientific thinking the

(Continued)

(Continued)

structures of narrative tend to be more codified and accepted as given (rather like the young child's 'all lived happily ever after'). But there are occasions when they should be challenged.

When accepted forms are challenged we inevitably confront questions of methodology. For example, presenting research through a style of writing that invites open questions, accepts different subjective points of view and embraces uncertainty presupposes a different view of scientific knowledge than one which emphasises the objective qualities of the material world. It is not mere chance, for example, that Randomised Control Trial results are presented in a formulaic way. Such trials are premised upon a view of medical treatment which reflects a similarly static and formulaic view of health.

So, in my thinking about narrative in academic writing, I need to be aware that more is at stake than merely writing style or technique.

People think in narrative. Our minds, when reading, seek for the story. We have to convert a passive sentence into an active storying one, for example, before we can fully grasp it. We seek a verb (action word) early on in a sentence to know what is happening. Readers relate to writing not as static object, but as movement through time: as narrative. They do not relate to writing as a thing, as only a series of black marks on paper or screen, like a wall made of an arrangement of bricks.

Writers of fiction and drama know that people are interested in stories, characters and ideas in that order, with ideas coming a very poor third. Ideas are abstract: people understand and relate to concrete things more readily than abstract. So the most powerful way for writers to get their ideas over to readers is through stories, or perhaps characters. The philosopher Sartre did just this, in his novel *Nausea* ([1938] 1963) for example. Stories to explain complex abstract ideas is part of the culture of science and mathematics: Newton and the apple for example.

If all dynamic writing, including the academic, is narrative, then it must bear the classic structure of narrative. This structure carries the reader's engagement from beginning to end. The central element of narrative deals with a genuine perplexity or uncertainty. We are academics because we want to solve puzzles in the world and cosmos, nature, human nature, culture and society. As writers we introduce our readers to this puzzle at the beginning; the rest of the publication takes readers on the journey mapped out by the writer to elucidate the problem.

Such writing lives in the present, rather than merely reporting past events and thoughts. The reader is therefore dynamically involved in something happening now.

Narrative Structure

A dynamic way to think of a publication is as a quest, which is the story of a search for something of value. Jason sought the Golden Fleece for example. He gathered a team of sailors, built the *Argo*, and he and the Argonauts set sail, undertook many trials, killed the dragon, got the Fleece and brought it back. Gaining the Fleece was a tremendous triumph and won Jason the throne, but was it worth all the loss of life and post-traumatic-stress disorder, etc.?

Like Jason, we academic writers collect our readers in the introduction and brief them, giving them the main thrust of the argument. We do not outline all the dangers along the way, or they might desert immediately. Instead we give them enough enticing details and information to encourage them to set sail with us on the journey of reading our paper. A succinct and helpful beginning to the introduction is one sentence which sums up what the paper is about, what the aim and focus of the quest is. This needs to be the first sentence of the introduction and the whole publication. Here is science writer Deborah Blum:

> I used to play a game with myself ... I'd write the first paragraph and then I'd put my hand over everything but the first sentence. And I'd say to myself 'Would I want to read the second sentence?' And if it didn't seduce me into the story, then I'd start over. ... I think the point of an opening line is to make the reader want to read the next one. I also like the way it can set tone, voice, foreshadow the style of a piece. (Blum, 2013)

With the focus provided by a clear introduction, our readers now have the confidence to travel through the elements we've told them to expect; though each section will itself contain surprises and lead to further questions. Each element is heralded by a subheading which has already been flagged in the introduction, or even the abstract. We conclude by debriefing readers, telling them clearly what has been learned or gained of value, what some of the major drawbacks were, and give them a few pointers for their next adventure. The conclusion uses names and descriptors of significant elements consistent with those used in the abstract, introduction and body of the publication.

A narrative flow will take the reader through from introduction to conclusion. The reader's interest is held consistently by new information, interestingly presented. If the interest is at all likely to flag, it is held by a sense that there is more to come (in fiction this would be a pleasing feeling of suspense). Readers' critical faculties are further engaged by discussions of authors' own critique of their argument or method strategy along the way.

What is Narrative?

By narrative I mean a confident handling of the material so that it flows naturally from beginning to end, taking the reader on an adventure, the form of which they recognise. I do not mean what I call a 'bed to bed' account. Little children when they begin to write stories start off with the hero waking up in bed, then they do something (clean their teeth, have breakfast), then do something else, and then eventually – they go to bed again. This kind of sequential and then ... and then ... and then ... is not a narrative handling of argument, data and theory, but a boring rehearsal of events, certain to be rejected by peer reviewers.

Stephen

Research into children's writing shows that by the age of 7 to 9, most children find such stories unsatisfying. Perhaps academics find it more difficult to make progress in the development of their narrative styles.

Take a tip from fiction writing. A short story has to hook the reader from the start, and keep their attention at quite a pace. Stories often begin with the vital happening, and then return later, once the reader is solidly interested, to fill in the detail. Many academic and professional publications bore on with background detail from the start. They lose me as reader; or else I skip all that and skim over to see if it gets interesting later. If this information material is shifted to later in the publication, authors find they needed much less than they had originally thought. We tend to begin writing in this way at Phase 1, as it is our way of getting into it; it is essential detail rather than boring to us. But just because it's a good order to draft material in (Phase 1), doesn't mean it's a good order for the reader: it needs redrafting in Phase 2.

A paper which doesn't introduce readers to the subject at all is a disaster. I recently peer-reviewed a paper which did just this: it had no introduction, but threw readers straight into the boring details. The writer had paid no attention to structure at all, taking no care of his readers.

We take readers by the hand and conduct them carefully through our material. Two powerfully communicative parts of any publication are the introduction and the conclusion, but I find it useful to do them together, last. Spending ages working on the introduction initially can create a block to writing the rest of the paper. If I know I'm reconsidering them both later, I can draft roughly, and then redraft once I am a clearer about the content and form of the whole publication. Why do I redraft them both together at the end? If I think of my publication as a circle rather than a piece of string, I want to bring the end back towards where I started, to give a sense of wholeness and completion.

The Structure of an Academic Paper

Now I look at the organisation of other papers in my chosen journal: different disciplines, and different fields within them, expect different formats. Here is a fairly standard outline format (often called IMRaD: Introduction, Methods, Results and Discussion; I have included Abstract). Handled imaginatively, it can be a narrative form:

Title	Noticeable, brief and graphic
	A subtitle can be lengthier and offer greater information
Abstract	Inspirational and eye-catching
	Persuasive and enticing
	Sums up whole paper in initial sentence
	Gives information on main theory and argument
	Provides location in the field
	Authoritative, clear, succinct, definite
Introduction	Attention grabbing, concise and to the point
	Theory stated clearly and simply
	Information on form
	How it fills the gap in knowledge/experience
	Where it fits into the field
	Why this research matters now
	Each section's main point, identifying important issues
	Poses *Tin-Opener* questions (Why? What? How? Who? When? Where?)
	Does not begin argument.
Context	Explains why this issue is researched
	Discusses existing research in the field
	Discusses what inspired this research.

(Continued)

(Continued)

Methods	Explains how research undertaken, and why these methods
	Details what was done, how, when, and with/for/to whom
	Discusses how similar research tackled by other authorities (if at all)
	Explains why this approach
Results/Findings	
	Describes what was found out
Discussion	Narrates what conclusions were drawn
	Offers possible explanations (why? and how?)
	Cites evidence from appropriate other sources (carefully referenced)
	Clarifies agreement/disagreement with these other authorities and why
	Discusses implications for any ensuing action
	Outlines unanswered questions and possible future research
	Suggests possible criticism of this research
Conclusion	Relates to significant elements in introduction
	Highlights main points, memorably and pithily
	Summarises argument fully yet crisply
	Points out strengths and weaknesses of study
	Is conclusive without being final
	Poses an open provocative point to reflect upon further
	Offers no new material
	Suggests ways forward from here
	Creates a thirst for more

These ordered subheadings can be referred to as a checklist of essential elements, even if they are not specifically used. This can help ensure we keep the elements of the Methods section distinct from those of the Results and Discussion, for example. The IMRaD template is not standard for many journals: Sword's research (2012) showed medicine to be the only discipline for which it was employed in 100% of papers.

Stephen

I like non-traditional formats for reporting research, but if you do diverge from normal expectations of style, form or method, it is important to explain why. In general, it seems that the more you diverge from what is expected, the more you need to justify your approach. Perhaps this is why innovatory approaches to presentation are so unusual: it's easier to follow the normal pattern. I have been involved in several journals where we explicitly encouraged non-standard forms, but we nevertheless invariably received standard submissions. Academia can be very conservative.

The very conservative IMRaD template is useful in itemising all the issues which must be addressed. Thus, even when I have reported a piece of empirical research using a fictional writing approach (which needs a good deal of justification) the traditional IMRaD form provides a useful checklist that I have covered everything in some way.

Checking the Narrative Flow

One effective way of checking the narrative flow of a publication is to extract and separately list a range of elements. I read this list on its own as if I am a reader coming fresh to my argument: does it narrate the story I wanted to tell?

First I extract and list the title and subheadings. What does the narrative flow in these feel like? If it doesn't work at all I know I have to rework them. Here are the title and headings from my final academic paper before retirement (Bolton, 2012):

- Who is Telling the Story? The Critical Role of the Narrator in Reflective and Reflexive Writing
- Introduction
- What is Narrative?
- Role of the narrator in writing
- Omniscient, and reliable / unreliable narrators
- Internal mentor
- Internal Critic
- Metaphorical narrators
- Reflexivity
- Ghosts and shadows from the past
- Why explore our narrators in writing?
- What is reflexive writing?
- Uncertainty
- The self as writer and reader
- Conclusion

For those who want to be meticulous, they do the same for the first sentence of every paragraph in each section in turn; the first sentence of each paragraph should tell the reader what the paragraph is about (see Chapter 8).

How to Begin an Academic Paper

Beginnings and endings of writing are significant as they might well determine whether a potential reader reads it all, and what they are left with afterwards. Most of *Inspirational Writing* concerns the middle, so to finish this chapter I'll focus on the title and the first and final sentences.

How to begin

The title attracts readers, who might be peers, editors or peer reviewers. Erika uses a metaphor to give power to her draft book title.

> My book title is *Lives of Models: How Mathematical Techniques Keep Us Healthy*. I found it by doing free writing, then I asked the book, slept on it, drafted various versions of it. My work has very much been about lives of models and I thought I'd need to get rid of it as I feared it's something too silly. But the book disagreed and once I got the title, the structure followed – it is a biography of the models, something I practiced in terms of facts in one of my papers. So last week I nested at home, hardly progressing but through these exercises found my way through to the title. Once it was on paper, it just feels right, and I feel excited about it!
>
> (Erika Mansnerus)

If there is a verb in the title, it is the most significant word, the doing word, and needs to be strong: the idea that mathematical techniques can 'keep' us healthy is intriguing. I have written, amongst other titles, *Writing Values*, *Writing Cures*, *Write Yourself*, *Writing Myself*, *Keep Taking the Words*, *Reflections through the Looking Glass*. Stephen's books are *The Enquiring Classroom*, *The Enquiring Tutor*, *The Enquiring University Teacher*, *The Enquiring University*.

An academic paper's introduction begins with a sentence which sums up as closely, clearly and succinctly as possible what the whole publication is about, while keeping readers in suspense about the significant details. This is followed by an outline of the contents of the paper as a whole (the Why? What? How? Who? When? Where?) using the subheadings from the text as guides to what needs to be included. Readers need to be told why, specifically, it is useful for them to read it. All this needs to grasp the attention of readers as interestingly as possible while yet being concise, and to the point.

The one sentence which sums up the publication, I call the party essential. I meet an intelligent non-academic at a party; they ask me 'and what are you working on now?' I've failed myself if I just stare at them blankly. So I practise for the eventuality of this question. And of course the sentence expresses what my publication is about to my readers: it is a draft of the first sentence of my introduction and abstract. Once I'm able to draft this sentence reasonably satisfactorily, I know I am ready to write a full Second Phase draft. So I keep trying to write this one sentence, with no cheating with colons or semi-colons.

Then I write that sentence again for a totally different reader. And then again for another completely different reader. Here are Rob's sentence drafts, followed by Paula's:

1 My writing is about the importance of the social environment for the development of critical thinking in University students.

2 The social environment for students includes both teachers and peers, both are crucial for the development of critical thinking in University students.

3 The social environment is crucial for critical thinking development in University students. This thesis will examine the validity of this statement. I use a longitudinal study that focuses on student experiences of critical thinking development in an undergraduate Zoology curriculum ...

(Rob Wass)

Paula used the tin openers:

Paula's research will use

How: narrative inquiry (to)

What: explore professional development and professional identity (of)

Who/Where: college teachers at [Institution]

When: over their careers (in order)

Why: to identify the influences (enablers/barriers) on teacher development and to recommend modules/focus for initial teacher training and/or ongoing training.

[Here it is without 'tin-opener' words:] Paula's research will use narrative inquiry to explore professional development and professional identity of college teachers at [Institution] over their careers (in order) to identify the influences (enablers/barriers) on teacher development and to recommend modules/focus for initial teacher training and/or ongoing training.

(Paula Hayden)

How to End an Academic Paper

The conclusion brings the paper to an interesting end, while suggesting ways forward for the reader to think about, and possible new related directions for further research. It states what I think the consequences of my research might be. It does not boringly repeat what I've already said.

Like the introduction, though, the conclusion could well begin with a strong sentence. This time the sentence could describe the contribution to the field of the research discussed in the publication; the achievement of the research can be stated straightforwardly and appropriately firmly. All claims do need to be verifiable, of course. Here are Emma's draft sentences, the first for her introduction, the second for her conclusion:

> This paper proposes that postmodern, narrative practice approaches are best able to modify the idea of 'cultural competence' in social work so as it can be applied in an empowering way to people with multiple ethnic identities.
>
> This paper uses the experience of those who claim more than one ethnic identity, to highlight the shortcomings of 'cultural competence' models that presume neat, bounded cultural translation from one generation to the next. Such conceptualisations of ethnic identity tend to obscure power relationships, and pathologise those who embrace multiple ethnic identities, best understood as the improvisation of changeable narratives.
>
> (Emma)

This first sentence can be followed by another which perhaps describes what a further study might be. Or it might define my project more fully.

Stephen

As a peer reviewer or PhD examiner, I like conclusions which emphasise the speculative and tentative nature of findings. This invites me to take part in further thinking rather than me feeling hit on the head by the conclusiveness of the discussion. The best academic paper (and the best science in general) is that which invites further interesting questions. A successful PhD student of mine wrote about me on an Acknowledgements page: 'above all he has shown me that modesty and intellectual achievement should inevitably go together.' I took that as a great compliment. It was fascinating for me to observe how as this student (like others I have known) gained in confidence through the process of PhD study he became more comfortable with expressing himself tentatively. He was therefore on much firmer intellectual ground.

Consistency

Certain essentials inform and sustain readers, keeping up potentially flagging energy and involvement. Significant elements, let's call them characters, need introducing, and their names and characteristics need to be consistent. For example, I asked one writer to explain what is 'narrative therapy'; and what 'narrative based medicine'? Why are they mentioned in his publication? I initially muddled the name of a significant character in my first draft of this book; Stephen, my first reader, pointed it out to me. I ended up calling this powerful force only 'internal terrorist' (see Chapter 8), whereas I had initially also confusingly called it 'internal negative critic' and 'internal saboteur'.

Readers really are beginning to be communicated with meaningfully, both in content and form. In the next chapter we turn to a further vital, and enjoyable, process to ensure a strong structure and eloquent flow.

 Don't just read: WRITE!

Here are activities that will help you move from thinking about writing, to actually doing it.

1　Write (preferably on paper) in a free-flow way with no specific subject, for *six minutes*, dumping whatever is in your mind onto the page. Do it every morning for at least a week. This is also a very effective way to begin every writing session (see above).

2　Write one sentence which sums up your whole publication (more than one [semi-] colon is cheating). It might take a while, but it's worth persevering (see above).

3　Rewrite your one sentence for a totally different readership: first year undergraduate or complete lay person perhaps (see above).

4　Write one sentence which sums up your publication's contribution to the field, or implications for practice or further research (see above).

5　Look at your Introduction (if indeed you have drafted it), does it answer the 'tin openers' (see above)?

6　Extract and list separately the subheadings or chapter titles from your draft. Are they in the right order? Can you tell if they are? Are they sufficiently interesting? Redraft them if not (see above).

7　Read through your draft pretending you are your future reader after publication (being able to do this can take practice). You are willing to give up readily if the pace slows, or if you can't follow where the narrative is going. Note where you stumble, and redraft (see above).

And READ some more:

Abbott, H. (2008) *The Cambridge Introduction to Narrative*, 2nd edn. Cambridge: Cambridge University Press.

A lucid introduction to narrative, this book includes sections on narrators.

Bal, M. (2009) *Narratology: Introduction to the Theory of Narrative*, 3rd edn. Toronto: University of Toronto Press.
This is an international classic and comprehensive introduction to the theory of narrative texts both literary and non-literary, the way narratives work, are formed and are received.

Bruner, J. (2002). *Making Stories: Law, Literature, Life*. New York: Farrar, Straus & Giroux.
How do stories work? Psychologist and lawyer Bruner suggests new and deeper ways to understand them.

Sarbin, T. (ed.) (1986) *Narrative Psychology: The Storied Nature of Human Conduct*. Westport, CT: Praeger Publishers/Greenwood Publishing Group.
This book, amongst other issues, discusses the use of narrative in the scientific enterprise.

Thody, A. (2006) *Writing and Presenting Research* (SAGE Study Skills Series). London: SAGE.
There is some debate about what is, or is not, an acceptable form of writing in academic publications. This book aims to make this debate more manageable for those wanting to assess which of the conventional or alternative possibilities on offer is most appropriate for reporting their current research.

11

Structure

The most communicative publications are memorable because they are lucid. They have words which flow in sentences, sentences which flow one from another in paragraphs; the paragraphs in each section follow each other and these sections are communicatively ordered. This chapter describes how to achieve this.

Seamus: The way I structure a lesson just seems obvious to me, but with writing I often get stuck down dead ends or lose the thread of my argument. It's so much harder than just talking to the students.

Helena: Well, thinking of academic writing as having a narrative, just as much as a story does, really helps with knowing how to keep the reader's interest up. But I still find it really hard to know how to give all the information in a proper sequence with well-formed sentences, paragraphs, sections. Perhaps section headings are a bit like painting titles: tight controlled, yet imaginative descriptions? My chapters are still a bit of a jumble. I like to think people find their way round my pictures well, because I know how to help them because I understand the technical form and structure of painting; and I know not to include too much detail because that bogs the viewer down. I think I need to know all that for writing as well. I've only just made the connection with the structure of painting, and it has helped me to see what I need to learn.

Lee: My research is all clear in my mind. But I can see now my papers don't seem unified. Writing 'one sentence' to sum up my research really did help. And I know now I need to connect it all with argument, with 'being critical', and that is the same as 'narrative',

> but how do I make it seem all one thing when I write more than one sentence? And I need to learn how English paragraphs and sentences work.
>
> **Joseph:** The English are much more economical in their use of words than us. When I was a PhD student my supervisor always said my sentences were too long, my paragraphs needed reordering and my subheadings so cryptic they weren't helpful. I suppose I just have to get used to doing things the English way. I had thought I was being too ambitious in submitting to the most prestigious journals, But perhaps it's that I still haven't mastered the English academic style.

The most notable publications read as if they have sprung from the author's mind in that form from first draft. The reader imagines this eloquence is due to the writer's grasp of what they want to say. This lucidity, however, is often the result of careful drafting and editing.

A line will take us hours maybe;

Yet if it does not seem a moment's thought,

Our stitching and unstitching has been naught.

(Yeats, 1903: 18)

Fine-Tune the Structure

Fine-tuning writing's flow for maximum eloquence can be achieved with a straightforward enjoyable strategy. I say enjoyable because this is rather like a game; all the tricky writing stuff is done, I can now really grasp what I have already written and wrestle it into good communicative prose. The strategy is to investigate the formation of sentences, then paragraphs, then sections and headings, and only finally focus on the shape of the whole piece. By the time I'm satisfied (more or less) with my words and sentences, I'm much clearer about what's in the text, and am then much more able to craft the paragraphs, and then the whole, into a good communicable form.

Sentences generally need the important bit first and additional information later. Similarly the first sentence in each paragraph gives the reader a solid hint as to what the paragraph is about, the rest follows (just as an introduction briefs the reader for the whole publication). As soon as a new element is introduced it needs a new paragraph. Each section can next be crafted to begin with a strong straightforward sentence telling the reader the point it is making, and to end with one on how that section has progressed the argument. Each paragraph within each subheaded section can now be organised to follow the previous one, like footsteps one after another. Each paragraph introduces a slightly different element yet linked to the previous one. Each subheaded section can now be cajoled to follow a comprehensible route, one from another throughout the paper.

This strategy also assists me in perceiving what I can ruthlessly cut out. Advice from Jackie Collins is: 'Try to leave out the part that readers tend to skip' (2013: 16). Yes indeed. Throughout this chapter, I use the example of writing an academic paper rather than a book or thesis, because of its relatively short tight form.

Sentences

Good sentences are the start of every successful piece of writing:

> I hammer it out sentence by sentence and it takes a long time. That's what the work is, right? To make the reader think it is not hard to do.
>
> (Malcolm, 2011: 13)

Each sentence can be interrogated: what is it about? The main clause of the sentence gives the subject of the sentence. If it's not at the beginning of the sentence I ask, why not? For example:

(a) Our study looked at a cohort of 50 nurses at the City Hospital in March 1997.
(b) At the City Hospital in March 1997 our study looked at a cohort of 50 nurses.

Version (a) has greater clarity than (b) because readers need to know what is being discussed (our study), before they are told where and when. Here is the same issue in a more complex sentence:

> Although scales and questionnaires have been developed for monitoring constructivist teaching and learning and reflective education in universities, some of these have been quantitative and focused on student concept of learning in science and maths classes.
>
> (Lynley Deaker)

In editing this, Lynley realised not only that the lengthy subclause (Although scales ...) was in the wrong place, but also that she hadn't started with the subject at all. Here is part of her edit, which begins with a beautifully communicative sentence with a strong active verb (encourages):

A constructivist learning orientation encourages self-development through reflection, relevance and responsibility leading to lifelong learning. ... Although scales have been developed for monitoring constructivist teaching and learning these have been quantitative in nature and confined to the subject disciplines of science and mathematics.

(Lynley Deaker)

The meaning of Lynley's new sentence 'Although scales ...' is completely clear. Yet only the verb is different from the original draft: 'have been confined' said what she wanted, whereas the original 'have been focused' didn't. This verb is appropriately passive because Lynley could not know who caused the confining of the scales.

Lynley's original sentence began with 'Although', which shouts its status as the beginning of a subclause which should be somewhere other than the beginning of the sentence. Conjunctions such as 'however' are also inappropriate sentence openers. Stephen writes in the next chapter: 'Journals are pretty conservative, however, so if you want to act against convention, transgress well.' Had he written 'However, journals are pretty conservative', the weight of the sentence would have been upon the word 'however,' with its implication of contrast, rather than where it belongs: upon the strong statement 'Journals are pretty conservative'. The word 'however', furthermore, if placed at the beginning, would not have been doing its proper job, which is to conjoin two bits of a sentence. While we're talking about conjunction position, notice my 'furthermore' in the previous sentence: I could have put it at the beginning, but it would have been in the wrong place. Listen to these (the first from a published academic paper; the second my edit):

(a) In other words, although it is certainly important to weigh the consequences of an action, we must keep in mind that consequences are only one part of the total meaning of an action.

(b) Actions have many results, some of which are consequences we need to reflect upon.

The only advantage of (a) is that the verbs are active (is, weigh, keep, are). With my lucid edit (b) we realise this sentence is empty and should have been deleted. 'In other words' is a clue that this is mere padding: if the author had expressed himself well previously, he would not have needed a second stab at it. So the phrase 'in other words' should activate the editing warning bell. There is also a clumsy cliché in this dull yet lengthy sentence: 'weigh the consequences'.

Paragraphs

A strong paragraph has an introductory sentence setting out the main point, followed by sentences which clarify and expand. This gives readers support in knowing what is to come in the paragraph, just as a paper begins with an introduction section, a book with preface and introductory chapter, and a sentence with its most important clause. I find short paragraphs are easier to read. Course members have found this one of the most useful exercises:

> Being forced to make decisions about 'the most important thing' was extremely helpful.
>
> (Academic writing course member)

To check and edit, I go through each paragraph and highlight the sentence which says what it is about: the most important sentence. Is it at the beginning of the paragraph; if not, why not? I then reorder the paragraph if necessary, giving my reader a clear path. Here is a paragraph Erika Löfström redrafted from a manuscript draft by herself and her colleague Anne Nevgi.

Before: Theoretical framework

First, to explore identity is a challenging task due to the dynamic complexity of the concept. Further, the concept of identity is a socially constructed and dynamically changing entity, highly influenced by the culture, difficult to capture, and so diverse methods (e.g. self-report instruments, in-depth interviews) have been used to approach and to explore identity. People have multiple identities as a member of a group or a social class, or based on their educational, cultural, social or national background or positions in working life. In all these contexts, a person defines herself as 'I' related to others, in a continuous dialogue of identity as simultaneously unitary, multiple, continuous and discontinuous entity. As a teacher a person has an identity as belonging to a group of teachers with similar educational background and similar tasks and duties and not belonging to other groups like students or nurses and simultaneously s/he is holding a continuity of herself by past – presence – future alignments in narrations, and with shifts in I-positions as mediated culturally. For an academic, identity as a teacher may be fragile due to the main obligation and interest of being a researcher. Even in a teaching situation, an academic may view himself/herself as a researcher or a subject expert and not as a teacher, and consider his/her task to be to deliver information of the subject to students.

After redrafting: Theoretical framework: Understanding teacher identity in academia

The dynamic complexity of identity presents us with a challenge. Identity is a socially constructed and dynamically changing entity influenced by culture. Individuals have multiple identities pertaining to different contexts. Identities can be formed around group membership, social class, professional attributes and positions or educational, cultural, or national background. In all contexts, a person defines herself (I) in relation to others. Characteristics that appear paradoxical i.e. unity and multiplicity, continuity and discontinuity, have been used to describe identity. These characteristics make 'identity' difficult to capture and scrutinise. Various methods, such as self-report instruments and in-depth interviews, have been used to approach and to explore identity.

(Erika Löfström and Anne Nevgi)

Erika Löfström wished to point out: 'Maybe these paragraphs can also serve to illustrate what kind of things non-native English writers struggle with (e.g. too long and complicated sentences, too complicated expressions).'

Before: *What are holy wells?* Are pre-Christian and very ancient and have had their highs and lows over time but still remain, especially in rural areas, a living part of the healing landscapes. In Irish they are referred to as *'Tobar Naofa'* and indeed any place in Ireland which begins with tobar- or tubber- is often a hint that a well is nearby (though it also stands for Abbey). As such they remain a persistent TL element within the Irish landscape for over two thousand years. Traditionally they are a mix of natural and constructed settings, though primarily the latter. Clearly a strong pagan link in terms of associations with healing and water which have been superseded or perhaps more accurately absorbed into Christian traditions. This association with faith and healing in place make them representative of the kinds of symbolic landscapes noted in the TL such as Bath, Lourdes, Fatima etc.

Draft 2: *What are holy wells?* They are pre-Christian elements in the Irish landscape and their importance has varied over time. However, they still remain, especially in rural areas, a living part of healing landscapes. In Irish they are called *'Tobar Naofa'* and any placename in Ireland, which begins with tobar- or tubber- is evidence of a local well. They are found in a mix of natural and constructed settings, though primarily the latter. There is a strong pagan link in terms of associations with healing and water, which have been absorbed into Christian traditions. This association with faith and healing in place make them representative of the kinds of symbolic landscapes noted in the therapeutic landscapes literature. Examples include places like Bath, Lourdes or Fatima.

(Ronan Foley)

Exceptions, of course, prove the rule:

One thing that intrigues me is how to best construct a paragraph. As I understand it, paragraphs should have the most powerful statement upfront, with the rest as an explanation of the first sentence. I explored my paragraphs and found that generally I do this, but sometimes I don't. Generally where I do not it is at the end of a section, or the last paragraph in a paper/chapter. I suspect that intuitively I want the last paragraph in a section to progressively build a case that ends with, in the last line, a clear explanation of 'what next'.

(Kerry Shephard)

Sections and Subheadings

Now we think of the paragraphs in a section in relation to each other. The first paragraph tells the reader what this section is about. Each new paragraph develops or illustrates the argument, and follows on clearly from the previous one. If a new subject is introduced, then a new subheading would probably help the reader follow the flow of the argument. This sounds obvious, yet many academic publications have random collections of paragraphs.

The internal logic of each section, and its consistency with its subheading title, needs to elucidate, elaborate and illustrate the argument and theory, methods and findings. The introduction and conclusion are particularly vital and need great care. The final sentences of each section summarise, pointing the way forward to the next section.

Section headings are signposts to readers. Sections need to make narrative sense so they draw readers along, following clearly the development of the argument and the story of the methodology, methods, findings and discussion. A good editing question to ask is: do the section headings alone tell a story? Making a list of all the subheadings, and reading it separately, can indicate whether the sections are appropriately titled and appropriately ordered.

If in Doubt Cut it Out

Sentences, or even paragraphs, sometimes prove really difficult to edit for clarity and succinctness. I discovered fairly early on that the best thing to do with these troublemakers is just delete the whole obstructive thing.

My first readers have on occasion recommended I cut out an element, and I've resisted. A tip from poetry writing is that we can sometimes cling for purely personal reasons to stuff we've written. I now find it worth heeding my trusted first readers, and try to find out why those words are so important to me. Here are two science writers, on the subject:

> [I leave out as much as I] can, but no more. And the meaning of 'no more' depends a lot on your audience, and the type of writing you're taking on. ...
> The less specialist your audience, the more you need to leave out, especially

133

the jargon. Remember that scientific terms that you use every day may mean little to ordinary people. ... You have to be able to simplify, to lose some of the detail that *technically* makes your piece less correct, if you're to achieve the bigger goal of communicating something that is right enough to a broad audience. At the Science Online conference this year, Kate Prengaman came up with a wonderful analogy: science writing is a bit like cartography. When you're making a map, you have to leave detail out, otherwise your map is ... useless to anyone. How much you leave out depends on who, and what, your map is for. (Henderson, 2013)

[I] usually [leave out] information that takes the reader on a side-trip. ... Sometimes I'll discover these amazingly cool facts or stories while I'm doing the research and I'll want to include them but, sigh, I'll realise that they are a side-trip from that main journey. And you really have to decide as a writer how many side-trips your reader is willing to take before they just give up on your point. When I teach science writing, I remind my students that science is, at its heart, a human inquiry, just people trying to understand the world around us. And that if we fail to convey that, we aren't really doing justice to what makes it so difficult, so fascinating, and so important. (Blum, 2013)

Stephen

I'm reminded here of Winston Churchill, quoting Blaise Pascal, apologising for writing a long speech, saying he didn't have time to write a short one. The task of rigorously editing out unnecessary words is invariably worthwhile. As a reviewer, I just get bored by unnecessarily wordy articles. I suspect I often reject papers that might have been acceptable had they been edited and reduced so I could stay engaged. It's difficult to overemphasise the extent to which refereeing is a subjective process: the writer needs to do everything they can to win the reader's support.

Is Everything of Importance Included? A Checklist

The tin openers are a way of ensuring I've included all essentials with a good narrative flow.

What do I want to tell my reader? Have I made it crystal clear how things were done, by whom, when, where, with whom? How have I set all this out: as a boring bed-to-bed account (see above) or as a dynamic narrative including only essential details?

And then WHY? Constantly asking why of every element in a publication at this stage helps to develop the intellectual level of the argument. Why is this here? Why do I think the reader will be interested? How much more information do they need to understand it properly? Here are some pushy question frames to help with redrafting:

- Why is my text a valuable contribution to the field?
- How is it innovative?
- In what way is it rigorous?
- What is reported? Why, where, how, when and with whom?
- Who is it fine-tuned to communicate with?
- Does the narrative flow to draw the reader forward?
- How are examples/quotes/tables/figures helpful?
- Are theories/data/events/people clearly introduced and followed through?
- Are images and metaphors fresh and original, helping readers to grasp complexities of argument?
- Do quotes from research subjects offer insight? Are they a refreshing change of voice? Do they illustrate without impeding the flow of the argument?
- Do quotes from other authorities support and develop my argument rather than stand in its place?

For example, if the study I'm describing is qualitative practitioner enquiry based, and I include descriptions of quantitative lab-based experiments, why am I including these? How is it useful to refer to research with such totally different methodologies and methods? What is my reader going to infer from this? That I'm muddled? Or that I'm clever in being multidisciplinary and drawing from eclectic sources? I must make sure I tell my readers WHY they are included.

The publication now flows, is comprehensible and communicates clearly: readers have been thoroughly looked after and will hopefully be so involved that they read avidly, cite and quote from our publications. In the next chapter we turn to the final writing phase: editing, an essential but rather slighted element. Paying attention to editing is not only enjoyable (I find it really so, rather like some people like crossword puzzles or Scrabble), but also an essential not-to-be-missed-out phase.

 Don't just read: WRITE!

Here are activities that will help you move from thinking about writing, to actually doing it.

1 Write (preferably on paper) in a free-flow way with no specific subject, for *six minutes*, dumping whatever is in your mind onto the page. Do it every morning for at least a week. This is also a very effective way to begin every writing session (see above).

(Continued)

(Continued)

2   Go through each sentence from the beginning of your draft. Is the most important point at the beginning of the sentence? If not, why not? Redraft sentences where the reader has to wade through subclauses to get to the point (see above).

3   Go through each paragraph from the beginning of your draft. Is the most important sentence at the beginning? If not why not? Redraft if necessary (see above).

4   Go through each section of your draft separately. Are the paragraphs in the right order? Have you told the reader what the section is about at the beginning before elaborating and giving examples, etc.? Reorder and redraft if necessary (see above).

5   What can you cut out, now you know your draft pretty well? Hone and pare to keep the reader's interest (see above).

6   You are a peer reviewer sent the publication you are currently drafting. Write your peer-review comments.

And **READ** some more:

Kitchin, R. and Fuller, D. (2005) *The Academic's Guide to Publishing*. London: SAGE.
This explains, amongst other things, the different ways in which social science research can be disseminated: in journals, books, reports, the internet, popular media and conferences.

Manchester University: http://www.phrasebank.manchester.ac.uk/critical.htm (accessed September 2013).
For a useful set of ideas and tips for academic critical writing. Although aimed largely at students, it provides useful strategies for the experienced writer.

Phase 3: Edit to Make Perfect

12

Edit for Posterity

Phase 3 pays attention to language detail to create an object of lasting value, a significant contribution to knowledge. Editing focuses upon getting the right word in the right place, upon clarity, order and succinctness. This chapter on editing explains how to engage critically with the words we use: how to handle jargon, the active and passive voices, when to use positive and when negative. The text should sparkle with the right words in the right places.

Seamus: When I teach, my ability to communicate with my students depends upon body language, eye contact and things like this as well as what I actually say. But in writing I don't have face-to-face contact, so how do I make sure the message is getting across, has the right emphasis, and so on?

Helena: I've tried really hard to be academically objective, but my first readers say I get obtuse and clogged up; can I really write 'I'? Don't I have to say things like 'the research was undertaken'????? And I wish I understood what metaphor is in writing. People say it's the same as in painting, but I don't see it. I suspect it's a key to expressing myself better. I do hope this chapter gives me solid clear instruction in the rules of editing, and what jargon is, and how it should be used (or not). And how to know when it's finished. I do find it useful to put it in a drawer for a week or even more, once I think it's completed. Then when I get it out – I can see it's not finished at all! But this could go on forever.

Lee: I can show my research to my reader now much more fully and communicatively. Now I want to get to what I thought was my only problem when I started: all those difficult English words, and the specific

(Continued)

(Continued)

ways you put them together, and the tenses of verbs. And when do I say 'he' and when 'she'? It feels artificial. When my writing partner reads my writing to me *aloud*, I can somehow hear the wrong bits better than when I read it silently to myself.

Joseph: I want to be able to write in such a way that people can really see that I know what I'm talking about. In sociology there are loads of complex and difficult concepts. For that reason, I guess I have to struggle even harder to be clear. I've been told I should always be positive, and that my double negatives are confusing, and to be careful with passive verbs, and adjectives and adverbs. That's what I want this chapter to do: help me to explain postmodernism in words of one syllable (the English language might need a lot of learning, but my English sense of humour's coming on isn't it?).

Phase 3 editing requires me to perceive individual words and how I've used them. The whole editing process powerfully fosters the clarity of my meaning, and its ability to communicate with my chosen readership. In editing, I enable my publication to speak to posterity. I want to give it language and form which will enlighten readers in the future, as well as immediately upon publication. Edited well, this publication will be cited, quoted, argued over, become a respected element of my discipline's canon ('as Bolton and Rowland say …').

Phase 1 enabled me to reflect upon what I had to say as fully as possible. In Phase 2 I redrafted to help my readers understand, to communicate my ideas clearly to them with a narrative flow to enable them to make sense of the publication as a whole. Now in Phase 3 I stand back even from that reader to perceive my text from a distance, to see it as an object in its own right.

Peter Elbow (2012) delightedly reminds us of the days when a well-paid man dictated letters to an underpaid female underling. The words he dictated would have been strung together anyhow on the assumption she would turn them into elegant communicative prose. In engaging in Phase 1 followed by Phase 3 writing we are being both well-paid splurging boss, and careful knowledgeable secretary. Here are three writers' response to these editing methods:

> I have gained an understanding that not editing properly is crucial in guaranteeing failure, and my not being able to bring myself to undertake a final stage of editing is about my fear of exposure, of being laughed at etc. But not doing it of course makes it even more likely I'll be exposed and laughed at!

I was impressed by how easy it can be to edit, but how *long* it takes!

I am a mathematician who loves rules to follow, so I much appreciated the set of questions to have beside me as I edit.

(Academic writing course members)

Why Edit?

Stephen

I used to think editing was boring. All those rules of punctuation, 'i before e except after c' and so on, reminded me of school. But now I think this internal 'terrorist', as Gillie calls it, has been pretty well silenced, and editing feels more like making my message powerful rather than getting it right for the teacher. I find the same when I endlessly practise playing Bach's piano music. Working out technical details of fingering and phrasing (like the technical details in editing text) are not really just 'technical', they are the creative way in which I make my own impression on the score (text) and make it really my own. So I now look forward to the editing stage of writing with some enjoyment.

Publications generally end up significantly more succinct after editing, without losing complexity, breadth and critical depth of argument. Editing does not focus upon brevity for its own sake, but on removing the unnecessary words, the baggage, which hold the reader up and keep them from understanding. It focuses upon the words which do remain being absolutely the right ones, in the right place, to give the maximum clarity, power and eloquence.

To do this we look beyond our individual readers. In Phase 1 we gathered our ideas together; in Phase 2 we related them to an audience; and now in Phase 3 we ensure that our ideas are presented in a form that will communicate across time and space. To achieve this we apply various writing rules and advices, so meanings and arguments ring out crystal clear and significantly critical. Research indicates that novice writers do very little editing, whereas experienced writers make substantial numbers of changes to the meaning of what they have written (Belcher, 2009). However brilliant research is, it does not ensure publication if the writing doesn't communicate. Some bad writing does get through to publication, but there's no certainty it will be read and built upon by the research community.

Stephen

I like breaking rules. But like many people, I guess, I soon learned that I need a really good excuse. In academic writing, rules and conventions can be deliberately broken to good effect. But transgression is only appropriate when it has a purpose. Then it can be powerfully critical. The most significant advances in knowledge, and in the ways knowledge is written about and presented, inevitably involve an act against some sort of convention. Journals are pretty conservative, however, so if you want to act against convention, transgress well. I find these the most exciting articles to read.

Style Advice
be more or less specific
avoid alliteration always
never stop being positive
don't use no double negatives
writers should never generalise
the passive voice is to be avoided
avoid clichés like the plague; they're old hat
typos make micemeat of the sense of writing
check the writing to see if there are any words out
exaggeration is a billion times worse than understatement
don't use more words than necessary it is highly superfluous
Jargon and semantic complexity can problematize simplicity of comprehension

Give the Writing a Rest First

Phase 3 requires us to stand back from our writing, to take a view from a distance. Yet in Phases 1 and 2 we focused closely upon its ideas and stories, upon being eloquent. To describe and explain well, I need to be close to the material. In Phase 3 I have to let go of the content I've striven so hard to make fascinating; I have to create a distance from the reader I've worked to captivate.

To facilitate Phase 3 editing I gain a distance by leaving my writing completely alone for a few weeks (or even better, months) before editing: I let it lie fallow. With this more distanced view I can perceive editing points clearly, for example, deleting elements which seemed brilliant initially but upon later reflection don't belong in this publication. With that distance I can laugh at clutteredness, clumsiness, opacity and horrendous grammar in my initial draft: *every* writer writes such infelicities, and needs to redraft them.

What does the Writing *Sound* Like?

Take a tip from creative writers again: read the draft aloud to see what it sounds like. Our tongues tell us when it flows and when it trips up. Non-native speakers find this particularly useful, as they might be uncertain about accurate English, but can become sensitive to hearing their tongue stumble over constructions. We are not used to reading aloud, and so might, in embarrassment, read with no feeling or intonation. I'm like this, so before I start I say to myself 'Come on now: LISTEN TO THIS, IT'S IMPORTANT!' I then am much more likely to be able to read aloud with sense, feeling, rhythm and clarity, and therefore pick up the congested, wonky or unclear sections. I've just read a section aloud and heard myself pause: 'aha a comma is needed here' I thought, and inserted it.

Wrong or clichéd metaphors can stand out when read aloud; it's too easy to gloss over them without noticing them on reading silently. An example of what would be a wrong metaphor for me is of writing as a 'tool'. Free writing is often called a 'tool' to aid reflection or understanding. Yet the word 'tool' is mechanistic and signifies a narrow usefulness, for example, a hammer has one use (for bashing things, whether crab claws or nails). Yet writing has as many uses as a cockerel's tail has colours (this metaphorical gloriousness is also in the infinitely various drink 'cocktail'). Reading aloud isn't the only solution though. A poor construction can be read with intonation to make it make perfect sense: for example, I'd better get it right how many people I invited, or I'll have too much food or too little:

> I invited the interviewer, Leroy and Frederico.
>
> I invited the interviewer Leroy, and Frederico
>
> I invited the interviewer, Leroy, and Frederico.

We can train ourselves to read exactly as it's written, and to hear better and better. Here is a well-established writer describing her use of these strategies:

> I chose not only the length of every sentence, but even the sound of every sentence – I chose the rise and fall of every paragraph to fit her – and to fit her on that day at that very moment. After I'd written it I read it aloud – numbers of times – just as one would play over a musical composition, trying to get it nearer and nearer to [her] expression ... until it fitted ... If a thing has really come off it seems to me there mustn't be one single word out of place or one word that could be taken out.
>
> (Katherine Mansfield, 1945, quoted in Gunn, 2013: 26)

Words

The right word in the right place gives clarity and elegance, going straight to the heart of what I mean. Our readers want to understand what we have to say, not have their wits taxed by our cleverness:

> It is not unknown to us that circumlocutions, exaggerations and polysyllabic words impress no one at this moment in time (the ante-penultimate month of the year), when I have a volcanically momentous message to impart.

We all have favourite words, and repeat them annoyingly; they slip into our writing too often without us noticing. As a book series editor, I had to read a manuscript recently which repeated wording such as 'she was the kind of person who'. I began to feel I'd scream if I came across this phrase again, and I knew this writer had not found herself a good first reader to be bluntly honest about the necessary editing delete button.

Stephen

I find it irritating when writers do not distinguish between 'method' and 'methodology'. The methods of a study are an account of what was done; the methodology is the discussion of methods used in a field of study and the arguments concerning their different uses, in support of the methods taken in this case. I often find that papers which should include methodological discussion only give an account of the methods used, nevertheless calling such an account 'the methodology'. The distinction should be clear: '-ology' indicates the study of something.

Plain common precise words with as few syllables as possible are often the best:

use, *not* utilise

now, *not* at this moment in time

based on, *not* on the basis of

Phrases like this are shouting to be rewritten:

I want to first briefly critically examine …

Sally-Ann Smith's campaign sired a torrent of media interest.

Her idea was seminal to the project.

Stephen

Gillie and I are often amused, when it comes to editing each other's work, to find that we keep making the same mistakes. One of my typical errors is the word 'clearly'. At first I thought this was just an unnecessary word that I perhaps used too often. But then I came to realise that almost always it preceded a claim that was either not at all clear, or not adequately justified or explained. Often I used the word when I wasn't sure exactly why I believed something to be true: it just seemed self-evident. For example, this statement in a discussion of student learning – 'Students' main motivation in their choice of subject is to maximise their grades' – might seem to be 'common sense' but, upon reflection, needs considerable evidential support and also conceptual clarification. Otherwise, it is not at all clear.

For me now, the word 'clearly' sets off a warning bell: an indicator that explanation or justification is likely to be missing. When the novelist Ernest Hemingway was asked what he thought was the most important quality of a good writer, he replied 'a built-in, shock-proof, crap detector'.

So when a writer uses the word 'clearly', often clarity is just what is lacking. In conversation, the word 'honestly' often has the same function. Why say 'honestly', unless one's honesty is otherwise to be doubted; why write 'clearly' unless one's clarity is suspect?

I think there are quite a few 'crap detector' warning bell words.

The strength of verbs

Verbs are the doing words; they energise writing. Listen to this sentence, the first from a published academic paper, the second my edit:

> This powerful application of stories can also relate to clinical supervision.

> Stories can also be applied powerfully to clinical supervision.

In my edited version the noun 'application' is converted to the verb 'applied': this contraction makes the edited sentence succinct and clear. The abstract of a later paper in the same journal begins 'The selection of literature for use in this research ...', instead of 'The literature selected for this research ...'. Nouns are often used in place of verbs in academic writing, particularly abstracts ('the interpretation of' instead of 'interpret', 'the conversion of' instead of 'convert'). Clarity and dynamism are gained by becoming aware of such nominalisations, replacing clumsy noun phrases with more energetic verb equivalents.

Tense of verbs

Within a piece of writing tenses generally have to be consistent. If it is in the present or the past it needs to stay there, or the reader becomes confused. In academic writing, however, tenses may change as the context changes. For example, Creamer and McGuire (1998: 73) begin explaining their research in the present: 'The purpose of our research *is* to identify the factors that ... academics ... with strong publication records *perceive* as associated with their productivity.' Methods and Findings sections are solidly in the past: 'we *were struck*' (p. 79). They begin the conclusion in the past – 'We *found* strong support' (p.79) – yet some of the ensuing concluding paragraphs are again in the present: 'Although engagement in this community of scholars requires ...' (p. 79). And the paper concludes with the conditional: 'Additional research with a larger sample of faculty *would* permit ...' (p. 80).

Focusing on the tenses when reading published papers can be instructive: how are they managed? Critically studying our own draft publications for which tenses we unthinkingly use is also a useful exercise (see Professor Pat Thomson on her own personal tense rules: Thomson, 2013).

Active and passive verbs, abstract and concrete nouns

Active verbs give energy and precision. Active is *doing something*; passive is *having something done to it*. People more readily understand the active: a concrete person or thing doing a definite direct action.

> I know the active is stronger than the passive.
>
> The passive is known to be weaker than the active.

Readers are less likely to grasp the meaning of a sentence with an abstract noun and a passive verb.

> We didn't know what the interviewees said.
>
> The details were not available to the authors.

Concrete language is so vital to understanding, that this is arguably one of the most important editing strategies. Abstract nouns (details, data, paradigm, theory, methodology) are essential sometimes, and passive constructions appropriate when no particular actor can be identified. If their use is as occasional as possible, the writing will be not only comprehensible but inspirational.

Passive constructions lend a spurious authority, yet are often wrongly thought to give a more formal, impersonal and academic feel. Here is Bernadette's experience:

> I remember feeling hurt when the first (doctoral examiner's) report informed me that 'indirect style and passive structures usually help authors to mitigate their presence as the protagonists directing the reader's attention to the research itself', and recommending that I replace first-person pronouns

with 'passive expressions and indirect language'. I felt as if, rather than having crossed the bar from student to academic, I had failed some important test – active voice might be engaging and 'fun', but it was not academic.

However, for the next examiner I had apparently demonstrated 'an outstanding ability to express complex ideas clearly and concisely' and my writing style was 'approachable, fresh and engaging'. The third examiner made no reference to the writing style whatsoever, except to say 'I thoroughly enjoyed reading it'.

(Bernadette Knewstubb)

Adjectives and adverbs

These overused words are only valuable when there isn't an exact noun. So I avoid adjectives when they have nothing to add: the right noun gives clarity and simplicity:

buttercup, *not* yellow flower

great dane, *not* huge dog

Adverbs similarly are less clear than the appropriate verb. Above I quoted from a PhD thesis:

I want to first briefly critically examine …

Here we have no less than three adverbs, which to make matters worse split the infinitive ('to examine'). Such a congested phrase indicates greater problems than grammar; the student needed to re-examine the whole passage closely.

Positive is stronger than negative (especially double negative)

Academic writing is too often stuffed full of negatives, often double negatives. As with passive verbs and abstract nouns, readers have to struggle for the meaning. Using negatives is a way of not stating too strong a case, which would make academics nervous. With a negative or double negative, writers can propose their theory or suggest a fact in a coy unfocused way.

I know the positive is strong.

I am not unhappy with the positive.

(See below for another double negative.) Here is a wily negative (from a draft paper): 'The role of the university lecturer encompasses more than the dissemination of information.' What *does* the role of the lecturer interestingly encompass? We are not told. The author was really uncertain at this stage what she wanted to tell readers. The paper hopefully now begins with a sentence informing the reader what interests the writer about lecturers' roles, rather than what doesn't. And listen to this splendid example:

> I am not, indeed, sure whether it is not true to say that the Milton who once seemed not unlike a seventeenth-century Shelley had not become, out of an experience ever more bitter in each year, more akin to the founder of that Jesuit sect which nothing could induce him to tolerate.
>
> (Harold Laski, quoted by Orwell, 1984: 103)

An editing strategy, therefore, is to seek out negatives, work out why I felt negative about that particular issue, and experiment with making it positive. By the time I'm at the redrafting stage, I'm generally sufficiently confident to do this. Turning a negative into a positive, unless there is a very good reason to keep it negative, creates a clearer and more positive reading experience.

Stephen

I'm not unhappy with this advice. But that's not exactly the same as being happy with it, and that is why I have put the previous negative sentence first in this paragraph. Since it is a double negative, perhaps it is an even greater error. Small differences of meaning, however, can be important, and there are times when the negative is the most important thing and should thus go first.

You're not unhappy with this advice, Stephen, because you are a real fusty dusty academic and like obfuscating with double negatives: I am for ever suggesting you edit them to positives.

Stephen

I think there is another reason why academics characteristically (and, in agreement with Gillie, I think much too often) start with the negative. This is because investigation itself is often a cautious process of elimination. One narrows down the field of possible conclusions by rejecting one after the other: 'not a, not b and not c, therefore it must be d'. Thus the research process often starts with the negative. In fact, an important scientific method (deduction) is to set up a hypothesis and then try to disprove it. As successive attempts to disprove it fail, then the hypothesis becomes increasingly plausible. If this process is transferred directly into text, then the meaning arises from the successive negative statements. This is exactly what we don't want if a text is to be easily understood, unless we want to highlight this elimination process. Starting negatively generally masks the issue, rather than indicating proper academic caution.

Jargon or appropriate technical term?

The *Oxford English Dictionary* (*OED*)'s first definitions of jargon are:

> A vocal sound resembling the inarticulate utterance of birds, twittering, chattering
>
> Unintelligible or meaningless talk or writing; nonsense, gibberish

A further *OED* definition is 'Speech or writing having many unfamiliar terms or restricted to a particular category of people or occupation.' Academic writers have to ask themselves if all their terms are comprehensible to all potential readers, or if some (or many) terms are so restricted they resemble the 'twittering of birds' to most readers. This self-questioning is particularly vital for any non- or multidisciplinary publication. A more everyday word with a similar enough meaning to jargon will more clearly communicate. Michael Billig complains that social scientists write 'like academic advertisers' (2013: 5), and:

> Academics are producing hastily written works. As the old saying goes easy writing makes hard reading. ... It is not merely the style which suffers, but so also does the content. When writing for audiences of specialists, it is easier and certainly speedier to reach for the common technical terminology, than to try to clarify one's thoughts. (Billig, 2013: 6)

Stephen

Everybody is against jargon. But I have found it really interesting when groups of academics from across different disciplines read a text from a field with which some are familiar and others are not. People are more inclined to describe an article as being 'jargon' when they are unfamiliar with the field. That may be because one becomes acclimatised to the jargon of one's own field. But it may, on the other hand, be that the unfamiliar reader is unaware of the fine distinctions that underlie the specialist words in a field and thus wrongly attribute them as jargon.

To make matters more complicated, technical terms are often used as 'markers' that the writer identifies with a particular perspective, ideology or theoretical position. That is fine if the specialist meaning is required in the context, but if a more everyday word will suffice, it can be just irritating. For example, social scientists over the last two decades have often written 'deconstruction', an excellent technical term used to identify a specific analytic approach, when the more everyday 'interpretation' is all that is meant or required by the context.

The test, as always, is 'can I say this more simply without loss of meaning?'

Here's a classic academic sentence, and a redraft:

> The deconstruction of data never failed to be utilised by the researcher.

> I always used my interpretations of the data.

There's a lot happening in this sentence. The verb, 'to be utilised', is passive and much clumsier than the simple active 'used'. 'Deconstruction' is jargon; 'interpretations' is intelligible to everyone. The negative 'never failed', can be replaced by 'always', a clear responsible positive. And finally, the reader of the first sentence is left wondering who on earth 'the researcher' is? Whereas after editing, the use of the simple but powerful 'I' means the author takes full responsibility.

Abbreviation

The full wording needs to be used, for clarity, when a term is first used in the text, with the abbreviation following in brackets. The abbreviation can then be used alone.

> Royal College of General Practitioners (RCGP); thereafter RCGP.

First or third person

Authors do have a choice about the way they address readers, order data, and construct and order arguments and theories, and they certainly have a choice in the way they create abstracts, introductions and conclusions. In Chapter 10 we introduced the structure and form of an academic publication as having a narrative, a logically constructed order from beginning to end which carries the reader through, so they don't give up confused part way through.

This narrative may be told from the point of view of first person 'I' or 'we', or third person 'the author(s)', or in abstract form 'It was found that …'. Whichever of these is chosen, that 'I', 'it' or 'author' is the narrator of the publication.

Which of these is chosen indicates the level of personal authority and engagement. Saying 'it was found that …' or 'the author discovered …' gives a sense of objectivity and authority which may not be justified. It is a popular misconception that scientific enquiry has to be narrated in such an impersonal form, as appropriate to its objectivist methodology. Yet attempting to avoid first person pronouns can lead to confused roundabout constructions. 'The author' instead of 'I' can mark a paper out as written by a beginner. 'It is thought' or 'it is considered' are even worse: who is this 'it' which does so much thinking?

If 'I' is used, it is the scholarly self, the narrator of a scholarly piece of work. This scholarly voice constructs and communicates the argument, presents the data and findings and relates all this to the appropriate disciplinary field.

The academic first person singular is not the same 'I' as the author who does, feels and thinks all sorts of personal things. Readers are not interested in the author as a person. For example readers will reject any statement beginning 'I believe ...', because they are not interested in personal views, but in the significant contribution to knowledge that the scholarly 'I' (the narrator) has to communicate about her/his research, and its implications.

Being able to create this narrator, and to wield it effectively in dialogue with readers, is perhaps one of the most critical processes a writer undergoes. This is true for a writer of any genre, but is particularly difficult for the academic writer to grasp and then handle with authority. The confident scholarly 'I' or 'we' takes full responsibility for their theories and findings. Authorities, such as Sword (2012), who have researched this across a significant dataset of peer-reviewed journal papers, have found that authors consistently use 'I' and 'we', especially in the natural sciences, contrary to the above misconception.

Stephen

I think much so-called academic writing portrays a false sense of objectivity and truth. For example, 'it was observed to be the case that this happened' sounds scientific or objective; 'I observed that this happened' sounds subjective and therefore might have been mistaken. Beginner academic writers are even taught to use such awkward phrases to make their writing seem scientific. Not only is clarity thereby lost, but the reader is likely to lose their trust in a text which tries hard to pretend objectivity. If avoiding mistakes in observation, for example, is important, then methods should be used to check upon observations.

Joan had a powerful experience of discovering vital new avenues when she had to rewrite as 'I'.

I decided to re-write the thesis in the 1st person as one way of addressing the examiners' feedback which suggested the thesis appeared too clinical. Among other things, by writing in the third person, I had appeared to distance myself from the research to the extent that they felt I was closer to working in the positivist paradigm.

I then found I had a lot to say that had always remained silent. To go back to how I saw the world as a child, as a West Indian, as a gay person, was the start of me developing my voice and weaving me and my story through the text. It felt very frightening and I felt very vulnerable 'exposing' myself to supervisors who knew very little about me. I had hidden a lot of myself in order to present a knowledgeable person in control and clever enough to do a PhD, and they had not asked the probing questions.

Using the word 'I' helped me to make appropriate links with my world view and recognise more clearly the impact I had on what I had decided to do. I was now a real person with influence and a voice. I could engage in the academic conversations with authors in the field, I could bring my personality and perspectives to the fore through examining my experience in the light of what the literature suggests. I was 'ME', not some distant observer of what was being said making seemingly detached comments. How did I miss this wonderful opportunity during my journey towards my first submission?

(Joan)

Gendered language

Being aware of gender bias, and the clumsiness which avoiding it can cause, is a juggling act in which dropping the balls is too easy. Do I use 'he' or 'she' or 'they'? Or do I use them alternately? Does it seem more sexist to use only 'she' or only 'he'? I have in the past had my cleverly non-gendered 'they' replaced by 'he' by editors, because the case of pronouns has to agree with the following verb.

Certain words are inherently gender biased. I have seen 'sired', and 'seminal' in academic publications, both with reference to women. 'Germinal' seems a good ungendered replacement for 'seminal'. I've only just come across the 'sired' example, so if any reader can work out an alternative and tell me (via my website) I'll be delighted (dammed doesn't have quite the right feel).

Stephen

An academic I know invariably uses 'she' in order not to be thought sexist. But the subjects of his research are invariably teachers. For a male academic to refer to school teachers as 'she' is arguably discriminatory against women since school teachers are generally perceived to have a lower status than academics.

Metaphors and Images

Human minds find it easier to grasp things than abstractions. Metaphors are when an abstract element is described in terms of a thing, to enable understanding of the sometimes inaccessible world of abstractions and emotion. Metaphors serve as bridges between knowledge and feelings (Lakoff and Johnson, 1980). Malinski claimed 'metaphors offer fertile ground for nursing research' (2009: 311), using an earthy metaphor to make her point. Adrienne Rich referred to 'the great muscle of metaphor drawing strength from resemblance in difference' (Rich, 2006).

Few people realise how often they use metaphors and images to clarify abstract and sometimes complex issues or statements. 'Nestling snugly inside the skull' (Roche and Commins, 2009: 1) is from the second sentence

152

of the introduction of a book about cognitive neuroscience, written partly on one of my courses. This first paragraph also contains these metaphors: 'The seat of', 'hides its secrets in deep, shadowy crevices', 'clasping hands and whispering messages to their neighbours. And in this constant chatter of neurons, the electric hum of signals', 'that fathomless universe' (p. 1). These metaphors give a powerful picture, whereas if Roche and Commins had stuck to literal descriptions they would probably have lost many of their readers.

Metaphors and images communicate best when readers are not aware of them. I suspect nearly every reader of Roche and Commins's book will have their understanding enhanced, while being unaware of this clever strategy. Metaphor use, however, is not always positive. Here is Roche, followed by Mark Henderson, also a science writer, about the value and pitfalls of using metaphor in science writing:

> Sometimes there are simply no other means [than metaphor] available to convey complicated ideas to a mass audience in an accessible way. It is the nature of how we process information to seek to relate new material to things with which we are familiar. But we must bear in mind that even the most elegant and carefully considered analogy [or metaphor] will, by virtue of its use as a simplification, be fundamentally limited.
>
> ... Not only can they give a false impression of the nature of phenomena, they can actively limit and restrict the way we think about those phenomena as a result. They can shape the type of questions we ask and influence the techniques we use to investigate them, sometimes resulting in major aspects of a problem being neglected. Scientific analogies can be worse than passively insufficient explanations – they can actively obstruct our pursuit of knowledge. ... This has been called the *babel fish dilemma* (see Douglas Adams, *Hitchhikers Guide to the Galaxy*).
>
> (Roche 2012)
>
> [I use metaphors] carefully. They can be extremely useful, capturing an idea that would otherwise take many paragraphs of unwieldy text to explain. But they can also distort. Ask yourself carefully whether they are helping your writing or getting in the way. You'll often come up with a beautiful metaphor that, when you really interrogate it, doesn't work. Kill it. (Henderson, 2013)

We often write with metaphors unwittingly, they are so much an everyday part of our communication. So the editing stage is perfect for seeking them out to check their appropriateness, and if they are that dreadful thing – clichéd. I ask myself:

- Do my images and metaphors communicate meaningfully? If not, what other descriptive strategies could I use?
- Do they give messages consistent with my values? For example in this book I've written of keys and locks, houses and gardens, plants, and journeys. I

would not want violent or war images, such as are currently used in medicine (the magic bullet failed). Nor would I like to think of anyone hitting the ground running. I'd rather they took wing. Flying, they could travel up and down as well as along, and there's no ground to slow their winged feet. Flight means freedom: freedom to be dynamically original as well as effective.

- Are any of my images outworn clichés? Editing one of Stephen's sections carefully I found he'd started a paragraph with 'At the end of the day', apparently considered to be one of the most jarring clichés in common use (Marsh and Hodson, 2007).

Stephen

I think writers are often unaware of what they communicate by their metaphors or clichés. It sometimes seems that as soon as people enter a work meeting they change, often speaking an alienating and aggressive language, lacking the humanity and friendliness of personal conversation. Rarely, in ordinary everyday conversation with friends, for example, do I hear 'level playing fields', 'hitting the ground running', and 'changing the goalposts'. The idea of work as some kind of game with rules, procedures, competitions and so forth is a perspective characteristic of management. Sometimes, this managerial culture or 'discourse' infects people's academic writing. Researchers who write of 'hitting the ground running' are more likely to communicate conformity to management culture rather than their intellectual enthusiasm.

We're coming to the end of our shared writing project. The last elements of editing, and doing the final draft of the abstract are just as important as all the rest: we want our draft publications accepted by our chosen publisher or journal, and to be read, valued and cited well into the future.

 Don't just read: WRITE!

Here are activities that will help you move from thinking about writing, to actually doing it.

1. Write (preferably on paper) in a free-flow way with no specific subject, for *six minutes*, dumping whatever is in your mind onto the page. Do it every morning for at least a week. This is also a very effective way to begin every writing session.
2. Reread this chapter carefully. Every section is an exercise. Work through your draft with care using the strategies in this chapter. If any part of you sighs 'oh dear what a waste of time', remember peer reviewers are heavily swayed by good writing, whether they are aware of it or not. And remember, it might make the difference between your publication being quoted into the future, or disappearing into obscurity.

3 Ask your critical first reader to go through your draft also bearing the points in this chapter in mind to discuss with you.
4 Read part of your draft aloud, either when you are totally alone, or to your first reader. Listen for flow and its lack.

And READ some more:

Billig, M. (2013) *Learn to Write Badly: How to Succeed in the Social Sciences.* New York: Cambridge University Press.
A witty and helpful introduction to reducing the pomposity, and increasing the readability and accuracy of social scientific writing. The title is a bit too jokey, don't be put off by it: this is a serious text.

Crystal, D. (1995) *The Cambridge Encyclopedia of the English Language.* Cambridge: Cambridge University Press.
This is a marvellous reference book full of fascinating research and discussion about every aspect of the English language. Crystal can even make grammar the subject of a good bedtime read.

Elbow, P. (2012) *Vernacular Eloquence: What Speech can Bring to Writing.* New York: Oxford University Press.
Here Elbow shows how the way we speak can inform our ideas about and practices of academic writing, while also having a democratising influence.

Guttenplan, S. (2005) *Objects of Metaphor.* Oxford: Oxford University Press.
Metaphor is an integral and vital element of communication; its study is central to the study of language. Metaphor is a much researched and contested area, especially in philosophy, as Samuel Guttenplan makes graphically clear in this authoritative and dense book.

Ong, W. (1975) 'The writer's audience is always a fiction', *PMLA: Publications of the Modern Language Association of America*, 90 (1): 9–21.
This chapter introduced the theory that a good academic writer develops a critical scholarly narrator for their publication. Ong suggests that the audience, or readership is also a fiction.

Thomson, P. (2013) *Patter*: http://patthomson.wordpress.com (accessed September 2013).
This is a well-written blog in which Professor Pat Thomson draws on long experience to communicate a range of issues in refreshingly ordinary language, from managing wildly different peer-review reports on an academic paper draft, to what 'methodology' means, to how to reduce work stress.

13

Ready to Go

At the end of our writing journey, we return to the beginning and sort out the abstract. This is perhaps the most significant brief set of words that academics write; this chapter cuts through the confusion about what abstracts are and should be. Checking references and permissions are time-consuming; advice is given on getting them right. That vital, but unfortunately boring-seeming subject, punctuation and grammar, is made to seem interesting, if not fascinating. Now the whole draft manuscript is ready to be discussed fully with a trusted trusting confidential peer, which can take courage as it needs unflinching honesty. After the MS has been sent, a nail-biting wait for peer reviewers' and editors' comments ensues.

Seamus: I always have a problem with reviewers' comments. I dread reading them to start with, then I find that they often say wildly different things anyway. How can I make them all happy?

Helena: Oh dear what is an Abstract? Just as I'm feeling so much more at home with all this academic sort of writing, here's something which is a complete mystery. And I need to know about all those other tricksy things like getting references correct, and … Perhaps I should have stuck to painting? More rules of grammar for me to learn in this chapter: good. This editing lark, which I SO feared has now become rather like a game: like some people enjoy word games and crosswords, Scrabble and stuff.

Lee: OK, but I still don't know where to put commas, or colons and semi-colons. And I know there's some legal stuff I should be completely clear about, and I don't. And for the new paper I'm co-working on with my team, I think I need to understand about 'authorship'.

> **Joseph:** In my field, concepts and arguments are invariably complex and so I find it really difficult to write an abstract which is brief enough without it missing out on the complexity of the issues involved. And how do I respond to reviewers who have a different theoretical perspective to my own?

The Abstract

An abstract communicates with editors and peer reviewers; many readers will use it to decide whether to read (and perhaps cite) the full paper. It should therefore give the significant theory (procedures, findings and principal conclusions) concisely, emphasising new and important aspects. It needs to be so inspirational that it shouts *READ ME* to readers and potential citers. An abstract takes time to write because it needs to entice the reader to read the whole paper, while yet being soundly scholarly, and to stand alone in some circumstances. It needs to

- begin with the single sentence describing the whole subject of the paper (see pp. 110–11, 113); if I'm not happy with this sentence, now is the time to write a new one;
- give information about the main arguments and material, from all main sections of the paper;
- locate the paper firmly in the field;
- state what new contribution this research makes to theory and practice;
- supply evidence in support of the theory;
- meet the requirements of the chosen journal (including length and form);
- be positive and appropriately confident, not provisional, like 'this study seeks to …';
- be critical and not personal (e.g. not 'I believe').

Referring to all the subheadings in the text should give the main arguments and material. If the subheadings aren't sufficiently informative, they probably need redrafting, so that they not only do give this information, but also have good narrative flow conducting the reader through the text. The tin openers will also help: have I covered all the why, how, what, who, where, when?

Stephen

The abstract is crucial. In many journals the 'editor in chief' will distribute the article to reviewers having read only the abstract. Or they may distribute the abstract to prospective reviewers who will then decide whether or not to review on the basis of the abstract. So it has to be interesting enough to seduce the reader into reading the article.

Punctuation, Grammar

Finding the right punctuation and grammar can make the difference between sense and nonsense, between one meaning and another. A code like many others, they give clarity, ease of understanding, avoidance of ambiguity. Punctuation is vital, it's simple, it's worth learning so its correct use becomes unthinking. Here are my two most important tips.

- Have a good reference book on the desk, e.g. Allen's *Fowler's Modern English Usage* (2008).
- Reread a publication I've found enjoyable and readily comprehensible, to work out how the author has achieved this enviable style.

An academic writer might think grammar etc. doesn't matter, that readers will understand. Well, they might not: the positioning of a comma can completely alter the sense of a sentence, for example. Readers' perception of errors can affect their whole response to a publication, furthermore. The computer spellchecker is not reliable: it does not and cannot pick up everything (such as it's or its). Here are some more essentials.

- Semi-colons can add clarity. The bit each side of a semi-colon needs to have a verb and subject, like a sentence; the bit after offers a new but closely related idea. Like the previous sentence.
- Colons: the bit after a colon, as you see in this sentence, develops the reasoning of, exemplifies, or illustrates the bit before.
- The subclause in the above sentence could have been put at the beginning: 'As you see in the previous sentence, the bit after the colon develops ...', but it wouldn't be so clear.
- Semi-colons are useful. Sometimes, however, a full stop is stronger, creating two sentences. Short sharp sentences are clear, punchy and quick to grasp. Up to a point that is: you don't want the text to appear bitty and breathless.
- Exclamation marks are cheap and schoolgirly! Find the emphasis through appropriate words. (Exclamation marks *can* be useful to emphasise a weak joke!)
- Dashes belong in emails, drafts and handouts: use brackets, or (semi-) colons.
- Material in parentheses or brackets should be as brief as possible while still making sense. If it cannot be shortened to a few words, then it probably needs to come out of brackets. It would probably be better as an extra sentence, or a subclause following a semi-colon.
- When *it's* is a short form of *it is*, the apostrophe stands for the missing letter *i*; when it's about something belonging to it (*its use*) it doesn't. So: *punctuation is the academic's friend*, could be rephrased *it's the academic's friend*.
- *The academic's friend*: an apostrophe is required in *academic's* because the friend belongs to the academic. The apostrophe is only dropped when something belongs to it (*its*), to distinguish it from the contraction it's.

The common forms it's and its are both used in the third sentence of this section. Yesterday I visited an exhibition with a colleague: she could not help perceiving the artists as ignorant, because each time these three letters were used together, the apostrophe was incorrectly placed. A newspaper editor decided that an 'apostrofly' is an insect which indiscriminately scatters these small but essential elements (Marsh and Hodson, 2007: 21).

Stephen

I don't think I'm really a pedant, but as a reviewer and examiner of academic writing I find myself put off (against my better judgement) by trivial errors of punctuation and so on. The trouble is that once I have been thus prejudiced against the writer, I am less likely to trust their judgement and interpretation of their evidence. Once the reader's trust in the writer is lost, then the writing loses all intellectual purchase upon the reader. It may not be rational to conclude from a writer's incorrect use of the apostrophe that they are unable to remember what they observed with accuracy, but refereeing is not altogether rational.

Some Grammar
data are not singular
corect speling is esential
try not to ever split infinitives
apostrophe's need looking after
verbs has to agree with their subjects
only use commas, which are necessary
when dangling, keep an eye on participles
just between you and I, case is also important
to who was she speaking? It wasn't to an owl
prepositions are not good to end sentences with
if any word is wrong to end a sentence a linking verb is
every single pronoun has to agree with their antecedent
and however, sentences mustn't begin with prepositions
we mustn't write run-on sentences they are hard to read

Some of these broken rules, however, are now considered to be fine, such as ending sentences with prepositions, splitting infinitives, never using whom and starting sentences with prepositions. If any of the above rules are as clear as mud, get a good reference book (e.g. Allen, 2008).

Heevowr, smoe recrseah intadeics taht hvoewer we mdulde the lretets in wrods, if the fsrit and fanil ltertes are ccorert, msot ploepe sltil fnid tehm rlaley esay to raed, bsaecue rradees sacn wdros wlohe retahr tahn selpl tehm out.

Discuss the Complete Manuscript with a Critical Friend

The draft might be complete in my own eyes, but a trusted colleague might well notice elements I've missed. The final stages of preparing for publication are so obsessive that this can happen easily. The right person or people might be the same as those who read my earlier draft, or I might judge that my needs are different now. I make it clear I want them to be honest, and not just say, 'It's great!'; and I hope to return the favour later.

It can be useful to ask my critical reading colleague to rewrite a section of my MS in his or her own voice, a kind of translation having a subtle effect upon the content addressed (and I do the same with their draft). To be useful and no offence taken, this exercise needs lightness, trust and confidence. It also needs practice and willingness to undertake it wholeheartedly and unreservedly. It certainly helps both writers, even at this late stage of MS preparation, to have a grasp of the sound of their own writing voice.

References

A pruning knife is useful with citations: no reader wants to wade through piles impeding their understanding and appreciation. Readers are impressed by citations from the original rather than secondary sources, but not by lists of self-citations. Quotes should be used responsibly, rather than to replace the author's words. References have to be absolutely accurate and in house style; if you don't have a computer program doing this for you:

- Double check using 'search and find' to ensure:
  - all entries in reference list are in the text;
  - all citations in text are in the reference list.
- Check all dates, page numbers, etc.
- All *authors' instructions* for appropriate house style etc. are followed.

Permissions, Fair Dealing, Acknowledgements, etc.

I am responsible for my own words (as long as no publisher or employer holds the copyright for them), but as soon as I quote anyone else, they, or their publisher, may need to give permission. I also need to acknowledge others' contribution (e.g. interviewees) appropriately. Sorting book publication requirements can take so long that I give myself an extra two months when I set the MS submission date. Here are things I need to do, to ensure an ethical publication:

- Do I have signed written permission for all unpublished quotes, whether from students, patients, interviewees, etc.; does this include permission to use their real name or not?
- When I am writing a book or book chapter:
  - do I have publisher's permission for all quotes from creative publications (particularly poetry, even if only one line), and for all epigrams?
  - do all my other quotes comply with *fair dealing* rules? This prevents me from using another author's words to present ideas rather than my own words.

Here are the main points of SAGE Publications' guidelines on Fair Dealing for Criticism or Review, as an example of what all book publishers require:

> You do not need to get permission to quote previously published material, if it is critically discussed or presented in a review context in your work, and it is properly acknowledged, and of a modest amount. There are no set limits: it might be the whole work for a photograph, but for a short poem it may only be a few lines. What constitutes *fair dealing* is complex: it's always best to ask the rights department at SAGE. Here are some things which might *not* come within its rules:

> Epigraphs at the top of chapters – These *tend* to be illustrative, and therefore not fair dealing.

> Tables and figures: unless you are critiquing the merits of the table (perhaps in a book about research methods), you are really using someone else's work to present the ideas.

> Adaptations.

Stephen

Maybe only 2.6 people read each published academic paper. But the paper will be archived. Read by few at the time perhaps, any published paper is in the collective 'memory' for ever. This contrasts with journalism which aims to be read by many but will usually be forgotten quickly and rarely accessed again. This has implications for the style of writing appropriate for academic publication. Although, like good journalism, clarity is important, unlike much journalism accuracy and precision should not suffer in order to achieve immediate impact. An academic paper has to tell a story, but it is not a 'shock horror' story.

Authorship, and Publication Ethics

Co-authored publications are the norm in many disciplines, yet they bring problems mostly because of the very different nature and amount of individual contributions. Sets of rules and guidelines have been developed to cope with all this; they tend to vary with discipline and also institution.

Gaining clarity on all this can be significant, especially for junior team members wishing to ensure their authorial contribution is appropriately recognised. *Inspirational Writing* is a general text for all disciplines, so therefore cannot give advice for all, however. Biomedicine, for example, has very specific, carefully worked out guidelines and rules for researchers and authors. Having had several publications in *The Lancet*, I thought I would go there for my example of author instructions:

> We ask all authors, and all contributors (including medical writers and editors), to specify their individual contributions at the end of the text.
>
> *The Lancet* will not publish any paper unless we have the signatures of all authors ...
>
> In addition, please include written consent of any cited individual(s) noted in acknowledgments or personal communications. ...
>
> A conflict of interest exists if authors or their institutions have financial or personal relationships with other people or organisations that could inappropriately influence (bias) their actions. ... All submissions to The Lancet must include disclosure of all relationships that could be viewed as presenting a potential conflict of interest.
>
> (*The Lancet*, 2013)

The Lancet is a signatory journal to the International Committee of Medical Journal Editors 'Uniform Requirements'. Here is part of their Authorship and Contributorship section.

> An 'author' is generally considered to be someone who has made substantive intellectual contributions to a published study, and biomedical authorship continues to have important academic, social, and financial implications. ... Authorship credit should be based on 1) substantial contributions to conception and design, acquisition of data, or analysis and interpretation of data; 2) drafting the article or revising it critically for important intellectual content; and 3) final approval of the version to be published [These requirements have now crossed disciplines as the Vancouver Protocol]. When a large, multicentre group has conducted the work, the group should identify the individuals who accept direct responsibility for the manuscript.
>
> Some journals now also request that one or more authors, referred to as 'guarantors,' be identified as the persons who take responsibility for the integrity of the work as a whole, from inception to published article, and publish that information. Increasingly, authorship of multicentre trials is

attributed to a group. All members of the group who are named as authors should fully meet the above criteria for authorship/contributorship.

(*The Lancet*, 2013)

Rules follow on this website concerning which individuals can qualify as contributing authors (and which not), and which collaborators are appropriately listed in acknowledgements.

The Lancet also follows the COPE guidelines (Committee on Publication Ethics, 2013), which, although they are for editors and journals, can be useful to know about as an author. Complaints can be referred to COPE by authors, readers, reviewers, editors or publishers, if the editor/journal in question is a member.

A thorny issue over the years has been the order in which author names are listed. There are rules for this; Morris (2008), for example, gives a free online tool building on international protocols for allocating author order.

Sometimes author or editor order is alphabetical. This is generally the case on book covers, for example, though one I co-authored has my name second because my colleague (Jeannie Wright) wrote more of the text than me. I changed my surname legally many years ago, not wanting either my father's name or Rowland, carefully choosing my maternal great-grandmother's which begins with a letter early in the alphabet; I never regretted it. Some senior team members generously expect junior members to take precedence to help their publication record. Some senior team members, however, put their name first, despite small involvement in the actual writing or preparation. I had this experience many years ago, but felt that in the end it turned out well as my medical professorial colleague chose the journal, negotiated for it to take our paper and undertook all the business to do with it (or his secretary did).

Stephen

I nearly had a bust up with a good colleague and friend over the authorship of an educational research paper I wrote following conversations about our teaching together. He agreed to comment briefly on my drafts, but I felt the ideas were all mine and certainly the (at times painful) process of writing. But his name started earlier in the alphabet and so, he argued, should appear before mine. I suspect the fact that he was a senior professor and I an unpromoted academic may have had something to do with it as well, but he didn't admit to that.

Many years later, after I had been promoted to a chair, I had occasion to give some advice to a non-professorial medical academic about a paper he was writing. When he came to submitting it for publication he absolutely insisted that my name should appear before his as I was the senior colleague. The number of authors of a paper, and the order in which they appear, varies across disciplinary cultures.

Preparation for Submission

The moment has come. I really take my time now, and check and double check the MS is as complete as possible. I recheck the submission guidelines. The publisher's copyeditor even then generally gives me a long list of queries: we all make mistakes.

If the publication is a book, then the editor will expect it on my chosen submission date, ready to go straight into production. If it's a book chapter, then I send to the book editor, a colleague who will then read and respond, perhaps asking me to make alterations in keeping with the whole book. The book editor will then eventually send the whole book MS to the publisher's editor to go into production. If the 'publication' is a doctoral thesis, it doesn't need emphasising that this submission needs to be as perfect as absolutely possible. If it's a paper for a peer-reviewed journal, never be tempted to submit it unfinished to gain formative feedback. Reviewers might offer good critical help, but are just as likely to perceive this is a draft, and feel it is not worth their time doing anything but reject: the paper would not be resubmittable to this journal.

Final checklist

- Are all vital points/examples included?
- Are these points clearly elaborated and exemplifed?
- Do quotes from other authorities appropriately support the argument, without dominating?
- Are quotes from research subjects/collaborators accurate, useful, and do they have full written permission?
- Are anecdotes brief and clearly illustrate the argument? Are they fictionalised or has full written permission been granted?
- Does each section/paragraph/sentence start with the most important information, or if it doesn't, is there a very good reason why not?
- Is the language straightforward and succinct?
- Are boxes/tables/figures accurate and clear without interrupting the text?
- Have I followed *author instructions* for the chosen journal?
- Is it within the word length?
- Does the title-page contain my title, name, institutional address, word count, and does my name as author appear nowhere else?
- Have I written appropriate acknowledgements, *if* the journal includes them?
- Are any conflicts of interests, where appropriate, clearly stated?

It's Submitted! But Now for the Critical Peer Review

The hurdles aren't anything like over. Book publishers' editors will have a host of queries to be responded to (there's no need for me to offer advice on this, as editors and their assistants are brilliant); the doctoral thesis writer has the viva to look forward to, and possible rewriting requests; the academic paper writer has to read and respond to peer reviewers' comments.

Detailed comments by peer reviewers can be a gift. They might initially seem daunting and negative, but I've found it well worth my time and energy to read them very carefully and respond as well as I can and deem to be appropriate. The very process of revision they require always results in a stronger paper.

My paper is mine, however; it expresses my thoughts, ideas, research, inspirations: reviewers', supervisors' or examiners' responses should only help and develop my thinking and writing. Peer reviewers occasionally wish a paper were theirs and want the writer to rewrite it how they would have. I need to recognise and resist this, and redraft or edit the paper retaining my authorial voice. Before beginning on peer reviewers' responses, it can be worth:

- Not reading them immediately, but waiting for a strong time. For me this would be first thing in the morning, with someone I can trust nearby. It could be a disaster to read them just before going to bed, or even in the afternoon when I was alone and feeling short of energy.
- Reading them very carefully, and then immediately rereading looking for the positives and the possibles, because the negatives will have jumped out first.
- Asking my trusted first reader to read them with me, also looking for the positives and possibles.

Some peer reviewers, however, feel their job is to be like the old-fashioned teacher with their red pen; they seem to see it as an opportunity to be sadistic. These comments need to be discounted immediately. Some unfortunately see their role as being to state how *they* would have written the publication much better themselves: I had one of these for a book project; the book was sadly never published of course.

Stephen

Earlier I said that journal referees are invariably influenced by the quality of writing, often more than they realise. Nevertheless, referees will have different interests, priorities and values, even when they are on the same editorial board. As a consequence, a paper submitted may well receive very different and even conflicting recommendations from the referees. This can be quite disconcerting.

I remember a resubmission was invited with the usual request that the reworked text should take account of the two referees' comments, which appeared, however, to be quite contrary. The social sciences article had involved interviewing about forty subjects,

(Continued)

(Continued)

and subjecting a sample of eight interviews to very detailed textual analysis. One referee recommended that this subset be extended to sixteen to provide greater reliability. The other referee recommended the subset be reduced to four to pursue a much closer interpretation and more illuminating range of conclusions.

What was the author to do? Clearly the referees came from different methodological perspectives regarding issues of sample size, reliability and depth of investigation. After thought and discussion with colleagues, the author realised that both referees' recommendations could be *acknowledged*. In rewriting, the author stuck to his original number but supported this choice by a more extended argument. The journal followed its normal practice of sending the resubmitted article together with both referees' comments to one of the original referees, so she was aware of the conflicting reports, and took this into account in the final recommendation for acceptance.

Journals have different procedures around such issues. The story emphasises that referees' comments can only be advisory. Furthermore, the article is the author's, and any further submission is totally their responsibility. There will be occasions when authors feel unable to accommodate referees' views without undermining their own authority.

I have been irritated by some referees who respond to a submission as if the article were theirs and make recommendations for how they would have done the study, rather than helpful comments for improvement. Only a small minority of referees are like this, I'm sure. But one has to accept that the process of peer review, however admirable in principle, is never perfect in practice.

Where an author has not followed exactly what referees recommended, I ask myself:

- Have authors understood the referees?
- Have authors accorded the referees' views respect by acknowledging them in some significant way?
- Have they been clear about their study's limitations in relation to issues identified by the referees?
- What have authors learnt from the process?

Peer review is not only a gate-keeping exercise, but also an opportunity to learn from each other. Authors have told me they have learned much from the process, even when the final decision was not to publish. As a consequence they did not give up the desire to publish their research but returned to a new writing project with enthusiasm and greater wisdom.

Accepting Rejection

If it's any comfort, Rudyard Kipling had a manuscript rejected by the *San Francisco Examiner* in 1889 with 'I'm sorry Mr Kipling but you just don't know how to use the English language' (Henderson and Bernard, 1998: 56). Voltaire considered Shakespeare's *Hamlet* to be the 'work of a drunken savage' (1768: Henderson and Bernard, 1998: 72). And many Nobel prize winners, and other leaders in their fields, had their papers originally rejected (Campanario, 1995, 1996).

However hard it seems, now either this piece has to be recast for a different journal or publisher, or a new writing project has to be started. This new writing has to feel new and inviting for it to begin to live on the page from the start.

Stephen

Here is a list of common reasons journals give for rejecting papers:

- This is not the right journal for this paper.
- The paper is saying nothing new.
- The findings are not sufficiently significant (because too small a sample was used or the circumstances were in other ways too limited).
- The findings cannot be justified on the basis of the evidence and argument provided.
- Not sufficient reference is made to similar (or contrary) research findings.

Quality of writing is very rarely given as a reason for rejection. I suspect, however, that this is possibly the most important determinant of success. This is not just because reviewers are uninterested in quality writing, or are unaware of its impact upon them (both of which are probably true). It is primarily because the process of attending to one's writing is also one of attending to one's thinking. A well-written piece is invariably a well-thought-out one.

Once an academic writer has understood, practised and can implement fully the three phases of writing, they will gain confidence and a sense of academic authority, and their writing will not only shine, but gain precious citations and quotations well into the future.

 Don't just read: WRITE!

Here are activities that will help you move from thinking about writing, to actually doing it.

1 Write (preferably on paper) in a free-flow way with no specific subject, for *six minutes*, dumping whatever is in your mind onto the page. Do it every morning for at least a week. This is also a very effective way to begin every writing session.

(Continued)

(Continued)

2 Reread your abstract. Is it succinctly informative, positive, concrete, jargon-free with correct grammar and good use of words (if you don't know what these refer to, reread Chapters 12–13)? Does it encapsulate the main point of your argument? Is it going to spring off the page requiring editors to wish to accept the paper/book, readers to read the full publication? Does it begin with ONE sentence which succinctly sums up the paper? Redraft if not.

3 Reread the section on punctuation and grammar (pp. 158–9). Work through your draft, correcting as you go.

4 Ask your first critical reader to redraft a section of your draft in their voice; you hopefully will do the same for them. This needs a trusting and light attitude. This might not work for one or both of you, but if it does, it is a very illuminating process.

5 When you receive peer-review comments, read them at a time you feel strong.

- List exactly what they suggest you do.
- Reorder the list beginning with the ones you feel most positive about, those which feel most do-able.
- Weed out the impossibles (probably where they tell you to write what they would have written themselves).
- Take a deep breath and begin working from the top of the list.

6 You are a scholar researching your disciplinary area in the future: you are engaged in writing a literature review; one of the publications is the one you are writing now. Write about the publication you are working on now.

And READ some more:

Sword, H. (2012) *Stylish Academic Writing*. Cambridge, MA: Harvard University Press. Based on a critical analysis of more than 1000 peer-reviewed articles from the sciences, social sciences and humanities and the arts, Helen Sword's text is clear, funny and informative. Written with stylish panache, it explains, describes and gives vivid examples and imaginative exercises and advice.

Afterword

Seamus: What I've learnt is that when I write there is a community out there – not that different from the community of students – who are interested to engage with me in these fascinating ideas. Writing is now a social activity and I feel I've joined the club. I feel I've learnt how to contribute to their conversation; though not yet really part of it. No doubt that will come once I get my publications out there.

Helena: What have I learned, why did I learn it, who am I now? I've learned I can write, as long as it's in my own time and space; that it's not that different from painting. I've learned to write fast (Phase 1), and redraft and edit really slowly and reflectively (Phases 2 and 3).

I've learned what redrafting and editing and reflection are and that I enjoy them(!), and that I write Phase 1 best with the door closed, and Phases 2 and 3 with the door open (this latter is sharing the writing with critical others and really working to understand what they say and develop my writing accordingly). And I know that when I am afraid I will run out of ideas I return to Phase 1 again and scribble until I've made contact with my very real ideas and theories again.

I now believe there are people who want to read my words. I learned because I did NOT want to give up my PhD; I want to realise some of my dreams (I went back and replaced a comma with a semi-colon there). I am someone now who can begin to respect my ideas, and even call them theories.

Lee: I have come a long journey. I had to learn I have a voice. That I can write what I think. I can at times even write what I feel. All my life I've worked, and it has all been so clear to me. Now I know it is not so clear to others. I have to allow my work to express itself onto the page. And then to think of how to make it clear to my readers (there's no verb in that sentence, but I can leave it like that if I want). I can't remember

(Continued)

(Continued)

everything about editing: it does seem much easier and clearer now. It doesn't matter that I can't remember it, because I can reread *Inspirational Writing* as often as I like. And where am I now? My Head of Department even said I'm worth my weight in gold because of the journal where I've had my paper accepted (I wish I was bigger and heavier).

Joseph: If there is one thing I've learnt from this book it's that intellectual endeavour is useless unless it is based upon humility. I now realise that such humility is a consequence of real self-respect and confidence, not a sign of weakness. As a result I am now beginning to write in ways which I think might really engage people rather than just try to persuade them that I'm right. Though I still am, of course (another joke!).

Gillie and Stephen: Enjoy writing. Use it as a voyage of discovery and adventure.

References

Abbott, H. (2008) *The Cambridge Introduction to Narrative*, 2nd edn. Cambridge: Cambridge University Press.

Aitchison, C. and Guerin, C. (2014) *Writing Groups for Doctoral Education and Beyond: Innovations in Practice and Theory*. Abingdon, Oxon.: Routledge.

Aitchison, C. and Lee, A. (2006) 'Research writing: Problems and pedagogies', *Teaching in Higher Education*, 11 (3): 265–78.

Aitchison, C., Kamler, B. and Lee, A. (eds) (2010) *Publishing Pedagogies for the Doctorate and Beyond*. Abingdon, Oxon.: Routledge.

Aitchison, C., Carter, S., Guerin, C. and Mewburn, I. (2013) *Doctoral Writing SIG:* http://doctoralwriting.wordpress.com/about-us (accessed September 2013).

Albert, T. (1992) *Medical Journalism: The Writer's Guide*. Oxford: Radcliffe Medical Press.

Allen, R. (ed.) (2008) *Pocket Fowler's Modern English Usage*. Oxford: Oxford University Press.

Armstrong, M. (1980) *Closely Observed Children*. London: Writers and Readers.

Antoniou, M. and Moriarty, J. (2008) 'How can academic writers learn from creative writers? Developing guidance and support for lecturers in higher education', *Teaching in Higher Education*, 13: 157–67.

Austen, J. (1922 [1815]) *Emma*. London: J. M. Dent & Sons.

Bal, M. (2009) *Narratology: Introduction to the Theory of Narrative*, 3rd edn. Toronto: University of Toronto Press.

Barthes, R. (1975) *The Pleasure of the Text*, trans. R. Howard. New York: Hill & Wang.

Barthes, R. (1977) 'The death of the author', in *Image, Music, Text*, trans. S. Heath. London: Fontana. pp. 142–8.

Bartholomae, D. (1985) 'Inventing the university', in M. Rose (ed.), *When a Writer Can't Write: Studies in Writer's Block and Other Composing Process Problems*. New York: Guilford. pp. 273–85.

Bauerlein, M. (2004) 'Bad writing's back', *Philosophy and Literature*, 28: 180–91.

Belcher, W. (2009) *Writing your Journal Article in Twelve Weeks: A Guide to Academic Publishing Success*. Thousand Oaks, CA: SAGE.

Billig, M. (2013) *Learn to Write Badly: How to Succeed in the Social Sciences*. New York: Cambridge University Press.

Blum, D. (2013) 'How I write about science 2013: Deborah Blum', Wellcome Trust: http://blog.wellcome.ac.uk/2013/04/24/how-i-write-about-science-2013-deborah-blum (accessed September 2013).

Boice, R. (1990) *Professors as Writers: A Self-Help Guide to Productive Writing*. Stillwater, OK: New Forums Press Inc.

Boice, R. (1997) 'Which is more productive, writing in binge patterns of creative illness or in moderation?', *Written Communications*, 14 (4): 435–59.

Bolton, G. (1999) *The Therapeutic Potential of Creative Writing: Writing Myself*. London: Jessica Kingsley Publishers.

Bolton, G. (2011) *Write Yourself: Creative Writing and Personal Development*. London: Jessica Kingsley Publishers.

Bolton, G. (2012) 'Who is telling the story? The critical role of the narrator in reflective and reflexive writing', *Educational Reflective Practices*, 2 (1): 35–54.

Booker, C. (2004) *The Seven Basic Plots: Why we Tell Stories*. London: Continuum.

Bruner, J. (2002) *Making Stories: Law, Literature, Life*. New York: Farrar, Straus & Giroux.

Campanario, J. (1995) 'On influential books and journal articles initially rejected because of negative referees' evaluation', *Science Communication*, 16 (3): 304–25.

Campanario, J. (1996) 'Have referees rejected some of the most-cited articles of all times', *Journal of the American Society for Information Science*, 47 (4): 302–10.

Canagarajah, A. Suresh (2002) *A Geopolitics of Academic Writing*. Pittsburgh: University of Pittsburgh Press.

Carnell, E., MacDonald, J., McCallum, B. and Scott, M. (2008) *Passion and Politics: Academics Reflect on Writing for Publication*. London: University of London, Institute of Education.

Carr, W. and Kemmis, S. (1986) *Becoming Critical*. Lewes: Falmer Press.

Cixous, H. (1995) 'Castration or decapitation?', in S. Burke (ed.) *Authorship from Plato to the Postmodernists: A Reader*. Edinburgh: University of Edinburgh Press. pp. 162–77.

Clark, R. and Ivanic, R. (1997) *The Politics of Writing*. London: Routledge.

Collins, J. (2013) 'What a guy!', *Guardian*, Extra. 22 August: 16.

Committee on Publication Ethics (2013) 'COPE code of conduct': http://publicationethics.org/files/u2/New_Code.pdf (accessed September 2013).

Crasswell, G. and Poore, M. (2012) *Writing for Academic Success*, 2nd edn. London: SAGE.

Creamer, E. and McGuire, S. (1998) 'Applying the cumulative advantage perspective to scholarly writers in higher education', *Review of Higher Education*, 22 (1): 73–82.

Crystal, D. (1995) *The Cambridge Encyclopedia of the English Language*. Cambridge: Cambridge University Press.

Cusk, R. (2013) 'The book of self', *Guardian*, Saturday Review, 19 January: 2–4.

Elbow, P. (1987) 'Closing my eyes as I speak: An argument for ignoring audience', *College English*, 49 (1), 50–69.

Elbow, P. (2012) *Vernacular Eloquence: What Speech Can Bring to Writing*. New York: Oxford University Press.

Eliot, G. (1871) *Middlemarch*. London: BCA.

Eubanks, P. and Schaeffer, J. (2008) 'A kind word for bullshit: The problem of academic writing', *College Composition and Communication*, 59 (3): 372–88.

Evans, K. (2013) *Pathways through Writing Blocks in the Academic Environment*. Rotterdam: Sense Publishers.

Foucault, M. (1984) 'What is an author?', in *The Foucault Reader,* ed. Paul Rabinov. London: Penguin.

Frost, R. (1972) 'The figure a poem makes: introduction', in *The Robert Frost Reader: Poetry and Prose*, ed. E.C. Lathem, L. Thompson. New York: Henry Holt (Macmillan).

Geary, J. (2011) *I is an Other: The Secret Life of Metaphor and How it Shapes the Way we See the World*. New York: Harper Collins Perennial.

Gillett, A. (2013) 'Features of academic writing': http://www.uefap.com/writing/feature/hedge.htm (accessed September 2013).

Goodson, P. (2013) *Becoming an Academic Writer: Fifty Exercises for Paced, Productive and Powerful Writing*. London: SAGE.

Grant, B. (2008) *Academic Writers' Retreats: A Facilitator's Guide*. Milperra, NSW: HERDSA.

Grey, C. and Sinclair, A. (2006) 'Writing differently', *Organisation*, 13 (3): 443–453.

Gunn, K. (2013) 'How the laundry basket squeaked', *London Review of Books*, 11 April: 25–6.

Guttenplan, S. (2005) *Objects of Metaphor*. Oxford: Oxford University Press.

Habermas, J. (1974) *Theory and Practice*, trans. J. Viersal. London: Heinemann.

Hayman, R. (1986) *Writing Against: A Biography of Sartre*. London: George Weidenfeld & Nicolson.

Henderson, B. and Bernard, A. (1998) *Pushcart's Complete Rotten Reviews and Rejections*. New York: Pushcart Press.

Henderson, M. (2013) 'How I write about science', Wellcome Trust: http://blog.wellcome.ac.uk/2013/04/26/how-i-write-about-science-2013-mark-henderson (accessed September 2013).

Henley, J. (2013) 'Top tips for curing writer's block', *Guardian*, 2, 14 May: 3.

Hofstadter, D. (1979) *Gödel, Escher, Bach: An Eternal Golden Braid*. Harmondsworth: Penguin.

Homer (1996) *The Odyssey*, trans. R. Fagles. New York: Penguin Viking. p. 446.

Huff, A. (1999) *Writing for Scholarly Publication*. Thousand Oaks, CA: SAGE.

Hughes, T. (1982) 'Foreword', in *What Rymes with Secret?* London: Hodder & Stoughton.

Hurley, M. (2013) 'Straight talking', *Cam*, 69 (June): 28–31.

Kara, H. (2013) 'It's hard to tell how research feels: Using fiction to enhance academic research and writing', *Qualitative Research in Organisations and Management*, 8 (1): 70–84.

King, S. (2000) *On Writing: A Memoir of the Craft*. New York: Simon & Schuster.

Kitchin, R. and Fuller, D. (2005), *The Academic's Guide to Publishing*. London: SAGE.

Krashen, S. (2002) 'Optimal levels of writing management: a re-analysis of Boice', *Education*, 122 (3): 605–8.

Lakoff, G. and Johnson, M. (1980) *Metaphors we Live by*. Chicago, IL: University of Chicago Press.

Lillis, T. and Curry, M. (2010) *Academic Writing in a Global Context: The Politics and Practices of Publishing in English (Literacies)*. Abingdon, Oxon.: Routledge.

Limerick, P. (1993) 'Dancing with professors: The trouble with academic prose', *New York Times*, Book Review, 31 October: 23–4.

Malcolm, J. (2011) 'A life in writing: Interview by Emma Brockes', *Guardian*, Saturday Review, 5 June: 12–13.

Malinski, V. (2009) 'Metaphor: Creative energy informing nursing research', *Nursing Science Quarterly*, 22: 310–11.

Mansfield, K. (1945) *Miss Brill*, in *The Collected Stories*. Harmondsworth: Penguin.

Marsh, D. and Hodson, A. (2007) *The Guardian Book of English Language*. London: Guardian Creative.

Mewburn, I. (ed.) (2011) *The Thesis Whisperer*: http://thesiswhisperer.com/2011/06/14/shut-up-and-write (accessed September 2013).

Morris, S. (2008) 'New ways for assigning authorship': http://authorder.com/index.php?option=com_content&view=frontpage&Itemid=53 (accessed September 2013).

Nash, R. (2004) *Liberating Scholarly Writing: The Power of Personal Narrative*. New York: Teachers College Press.

O'Donnell, J. (2011) *The Research Whisperer*: http://theresearchwhisperer.wordpress.com/2011/08/16/shut-up-and-write (accessed September 2013).

Ong, W. (1975) 'The writer's audience is always a fiction', *PMLA: Publications of the Modern Language Association of America*, 90 (1): 9–21.

Orwell, G. ([1946] 1984) *Why I Write*. London: Penguin.

Paltridge, B. and Starfield, S. (2007) *Thesis and Dissertation Writing in a Second Language: A Handbook for Supervisors*. London: Routledge.

Peseta, T. (2007) 'Troubling our desires for research and writing within the academic development project', *International Journal for Academic Development*, 12 (1): 15–23.

Porter, S. (2010) *Inking the Deal: A Guide for Successful Academic Publication*. Waco, TX: Baylor University Press.

Rich, A. (2006) http://www.nationalbook.org/nbaacceptspeech_arich.html (accessed September 2013).

Richardson, L. (1990) *Writing Strategies: Reaching Diverse Audiences*. London: SAGE.

Rocco, T., Hatcher, T., et al. (eds) (2011) *The Handbook of Scholarly Writing and Publishing*. San Francisco, CA: John Wiley.

Roche, R. (2012) 'Lost in translation: The dangers of using analogies in science', Wellcome Trust: http://blog.wellcome.ac.uk/2012/10/29/lost-in-translation (accessed September 2013).

Roche, R. and Commins, S. (eds) (2009) *Pioneering Studies in Cognitive Neuroscience*. Maidenhead, Berks.: Open University Press.

Rowland, S. (1984) *The Enquiring Classroom*. Lewes: Falmer Press.

Rowland, S. (1991) 'The power of silence', *British Educational Research Journal*, 17 (2): 95–111.

Rowland, S. (2006) *The Inquiring University Teacher*. Basingstoke: McGraw-Hill.

Sarbin, T. (ed.) (1986) *Narrative Psychology: The Storied Nature of Human Conduct*. Westport, CT: Praeger Publishers/Greenwood Publishing Group.

Sartre, J. ([1938] 1963) *Nausea*. Harmondsworth: Penguin.

Stevenson, R. (2002 [1886]) *The Strange Case of Dr Jekyll and Mr Hyde*. London: Penguin.

Stevenson, R. (2012 [1883]) *Treasure Island*. London: Random House.

Sword, H. (2012) *Stylish Academic Writing*. Cambridge, MA: Harvard University Press.

The Lancet (2013). 'Statements, permissions and signatures': www.thelancet.com/lancet-information-for-authors/statements-permissions-signatures#authors-and-contributors (September 2013).

Thody, A. (2006) *Writing and Presenting Research* (SAGE Study Skills Series). London: SAGE.

Thomson, P. (2013) *Patter*: http://patthomson.wordpress.com (accessed September 2013).

Woodward-Kron, R. (2002) 'Critical analysis versus description? Examining the relationship in successful student writing', *Journal of English for Academic Purposes*, 1 (2): 121–44.

Woolf, V. (1942) *A Room of One's Own*. London: Hogarth Press.

Woolf, V. (1979 [1931]) 'Professions for women', in *Virginia Woolf: Women and Writing*, ed. and intro. Michele Barrett. London: Women's Press. pp. 59–61.

Yeats, W. (1903) 'Adam's Curse', in *In the Seven Woods*. London: Macmillan.

Index

Author Index